Legends & Lore of East Tennessee

Shane S. Simmons

Published by The History Press
Charleston, SC
www.historypress.net

First published 2016

Manufactured in the United States

ISBN 978.1.46713.638.9

Library of Congress Control Number: 2016934537

Notice: The information in this book is true and complete to the best of our knowledge. It is offered without guarantee on the part of the author or The History Press. The author and The History Press disclaim all liability in connection with the use of this book.

To Kealey, Sean and Will with all my love.

Contents

Acknowledgements

I learned during this endeavor that writing a book is by no means a solo project; it can't happen without the support, sacrifice and patience of many other people. I could write a whole chapter about all the ways in which my wonderful wife, Kealey Bundren Simmons, has helped support my writing. I can't say a big enough thank-you to her for the help and understanding she gave in making this book happen.

I also want to thank my children, Sean and Will (Joey) Simmons, for being my constant motivation and inspiration to keep pushing through to the finish. They were drafted into making some of the investigative trips with me with little complaint (provided there was sufficient Wi-Fi reception).

I would be remiss to not acknowledge the contribution of my wife's pet dog, Runner, who was my constant (though not always welcome) sidekick throughout the process—should technology advance to the point where dogs can read, she will be very appreciative of the mention.

I also want to thank my parents, Bill and Linda Simmons, and brothers, Billy and Ben, for helping to spark my interest in history as a child. Memories of growing up in the small community of Doran, just outside Richlands, planted the seed of appreciation for roots and the importance of documenting the disappearing Appalachian culture in which I was raised.

I want to use this opportunity to show appreciation to my brother in Appalachian history, Jason Barton. The encouragement, feedback and response from supporters of The Appalachian Project (TAP) have really inspired this effort. Your interest in learning more about our culture and heritage has been a major motivator in undertaking this challenge.

I also want to say a big thank-you to some people who probably have no idea how much they helped to make this book possible. First, I want to thank Travis Lowe for his sound advice of not overthinking and trying too hard to be perfect—don't make excuses and procrastinate; just do it. I also want to thank Rena McCoy O'Quinn for giving me the recipe to make it happen with a manageable plan to pace myself—a small gesture that was a big help, as it gave me me a workable plan of action. Finally, I want to thank Amy Pennington Brudnicki for giving sound feedback, encouragement and advice on my writing efforts. As is always the case, I know I am overlooking some people who have contributed to this book. I hope you will know it is an oversight of the head and not the heart.

Introduction

East Tennessee is chock full of legends and folklore, dating back centuries to the days when Native Americans roamed the area. Many of these tales, traditions and customs from the Native Americans have fused with the heavy Scotch-Irish influence of the early white settlers to form a most unique history. The writing of this book was a massive undertaking, as there are mounds of information about the area and it is quite difficult to narrow it all down to do the stories justice. Most of the stories have been handed down for generations, as many families in the area go back for centuries.

Storytelling is a very popular pastime in East Tennessee, as evidenced by the wildly popular International Storytelling Center and its annual National Storytelling Festival, held the first weekend of every October, which routinely draws a crowd in excess of ten thousand people to the town of Jonesborough. Much of the storytelling talent developed from the rural nature of life in the mountains, where other entertainment isn't readily available. Storytelling and music became staples of entertainment at parties and family get-togethers, where a roaring good yarn could suck in the attention of the entire crowd. Many of the tall tales and legends were told in this manner, which is why there have been more than a few embellishments added to the stories. The old adage "don't let the truth get in the way of a good story" is very applicable in this case.

In researching this book, I was surprised how many of the tales and legends were at least partially based on the truth. Battles between settlers and Native Americans, frontier exploration, tragic accidents and curiosities of nature have combined to make the mountains of East Tennessee fertile ground for legends and lore. I attempted to pick the best of these stories from the various counties in the area for this book—a difficult chore indeed. Like what seems to always happen with a "greatest hits" album by your favorite musician, I am sure that some folks will like one of the best stories that isn't included here.

My hope is not to have included each and every great legend from the area, as that would be quite impossible in one volume, but to have included stories that will spark curiosity in others to learn more about the area I now call home. I went into writing this book thinking that I was familiar with pretty much every story worth knowing about East Tennessee; however, once I finished the book, I realized how truly little I knew beforehand. I come away with an even deeper respect for the history and people of East Tennessee than I already possessed.

It was also a great revelation to discover how many museums, libraries and landmarks still exist to visit in person to soak up some of the rich history. I would encourage anyone to blaze his or her own trail in search of history, as most of the sites are very affordable and many are free. I hope this book will show that the stories, legends and lore of East Tennessee are well worth retelling to future generations.

Part I
Legendary People of East Tennessee

Davy Crockett

There are legends and then there's Davy Crockett, a frontier folk hero with a résumé so extensive it would be difficult to fit into a series of books. Crockett's life was cut short at the relatively young age of forty-nine before he could add even more chapters to his already impressive life story. One of the reasons Davy Crockett is so well remembered is due to his own talent as a storyteller, as he could spin a captivating tale of his exploits that left listeners spellbound and in awe of his experiences. He also participated in writing multiple autobiographies of his life, with accompanying embellishments of his many frontier exploits. Crockett once wrote that he had killed 105 bears during a single hunting season, which is just one example of some of the questionable claims in his writings. He doubtlessly led a fascinating, action-filled life, and he'd likely have been the first person to tell you so. Several popular quotes have been attributed to him that have added to his lore:

- "Let the tongue speak what your heart thinks."
- "Be always sure you're right, then go ahead."
- Annoyed by long-winded speeches full of fluff in Washington, Crockett remarked: "There's too much talk. Many men seem to be proud they can say so much about nothing. Their tongues keep working, whether they've got any grist to grind or not."

Davy Crockett. *National Portrait Gallery, Smithsonian Institution.*

- "Since you have chosen to elect a man with a timber toe to succeed me, you may all go to Hell and I will go to Texas!"
- "Fame is like a shaved pig with a greased tail, and it is only after it has slipped through the hands of some thousands, that some fellow, by mere chance, holds on to it."
- "I would rather be politically dead than hypocritically immortalized."
- "I would rather be beaten, and be a man, than to be elected and be a little puppy dog."
- Of an inaccurate exchange with a political rival for office: "Fellow citizens, I did lie. They told stories on me, and I had to show them, if it came down to that, that I could tell a bigger one than they could. Yes, fellow citizens, I can run faster, walk longer, leap higher, speak better, and tell more and bigger lies than my competitor, and all his friends, any day of my life."
- "I have always supported measures and principles and not men."
- "We have the right as individuals to give away as much of our own money as we please in charity; but, as members of Congress, we have no right to appropriate a dollar of the public money."

David "Davy" Crockett was born on August 17, 1786, in the little community of Limestone along the Nolichucky River in Greene County, Tennessee, to John and Rebecca (Hawkins) Crockett. The Crocketts moved quite frequently inside Greene County in Davy's early youth, as the family struggled financially through a series of misfortunes. A gristmill that John had helped operate with his partner, Thomas Galbraith, was destroyed, along with the Crockett family's home, in a massive flood. John Crockett eventually moved his family to Jefferson County in 1792, but this was short-lived, as this home was lost in bankruptcy in 1795. The family then moved to Morristown, where John built and operated a tavern along the local route used by stagecoaches passing through the town.

Replica of Davy Crockett's birthplace cabin at the Davy Crockett Birthplace State Park in Limestone, Tennessee. *Author's photo.*

Marker honoring the life of Davy Crockett at the Davy Crockett Birthplace State Park. *Author's photo.*

Inscription in stone marking the birth of Davy Crockett at the Davy Crockett Birthplace State Park.

Try as they may, the Crocketts could not turn around their finances, and this forced them to make the difficult decision to hire out the now twelve-year-old Davy as an indentured servant. Davy would work as a servant for Jacob Siler, whom he accompanied to the Natural Bridge area of Virginia. Davy worked for Siler for a few weeks before returning home to Tennessee. He was high-spirited from an early age and soon found himself in trouble at school for fighting with a classmate, and from then on, he began to skip school. Once his father found out about these hijinks, John was going to punish Davy but couldn't catch the younger Crockett before he ran away.

Davy began to once again roam the land as he left home to work for a man named Jesse Cheek on a cattle drive that would take him all the way to Front Royal, Virginia. From there, he zigzagged between farming jobs that took him into Gerrardstown, West Virginia, and then back to Christiansburg, Virginia, where he settled down for four years. By 1802, Davy Crockett was ready to return back to his parents' tavern in Tennessee, so he set out on this journey on foot. Davy finally made it back home only to discover that his father was once again in hock, this time to a man named Abraham Wilson for thirty-six dollars. John once again hired out Davy as an indentured servant to pay off this debt. No sooner was this servitude worked off than Davy was hired out to pay off forty dollars that was owed to John Canady. Finally, the debts were all paid from the sweat of young Davy's brow, and he was free to leave to live on his own. Davy had developed a good relationship with John Canady, so he chose to return to his employment, where he stayed for four years.

While working for Canady, the future "King of the Wild Frontier" became entangled in relationships with the fairer sex that could have earned him the moniker "King of the Love Triangles." Davy became smitten with his employer's niece, Amy Summer, who wasn't available as she was already engaged to Canady's son, Robert. Davy was part of the wedding party of Amy and Robert when he met another young lady, Margaret Elder, who quickly became his new love interest. He wooed Margaret and soon asked for her hand in marriage, which she gladly granted. A marriage contract was drawn up on October 21, 1805, but this wedding would never happen. Unbeknownst to Davy, his fiancée, Margaret, became engaged to another man during this same period and ended up marrying her other suitor instead.

Not long after being rebuffed by Margaret Elder, Davy was once again on the hunt for a wife when a young lady named Polly Finley caught his eye at a local festival. Davy faced stiff resistance to marrying Polly from her mother, Jean Finley, who felt that Davy was not a good match for her daughter. This time, Davy was apparently determined to make the idiom "the third time's the charm" more applicable than "three strikes, you're out," as he wouldn't allow Polly's mother to come between them. Davy and Polly decided that they would marry with or without the blessing of her parents and took out a marriage license on August 12, 1806. On the sixteenth of August, Davy rode to Polly's family home intending to ride off with her to be married in another location. Polly's father was distraught at discovering this turn of events and begged Davy and Polly to get married at the family's house. Finally, they agreed on the condition that Jean Finley would apologize to Davy for her rude behavior toward him. It would seem that Davy Crockett's later exploits on the frontier were tame compared to his tumultuous love life.

Davy and Polly were, by all accounts, living a happy, quiet life as a family when an incident known as the "Fort Mims Massacre" took place during the Creek War in Bay Minette, Alabama, on August 30, 1813. The Fort Mims Massacre began when the Red Stick Creek Indians, with between 750 and 1,000 warriors, attacked Fort Mims and won a decisive, brutal victory over the troops occupying the fort. The Red Sticks set much of the fort on fire and by the end of the battle had claimed 247 scalps. The victory by the Indians sent a shock wave through the white settlers in the southeastern part of the United States and served as a rallying cry for vengeance. Davy Crockett was one of the men who answered the call to fight the Indians and enlisted as a scout on September 20, 1813, in the Second Regiment of Volunteer Mounted Riflemen. Crockett ended up killing more animals on hunts for food than any Indians in this first foray into the military. He then returned home on December 24, 1813, after serving his ninety-day enlistment.

The War of 1812 had dragged out into 1814, and General Andrew Jackson requested support from the Tennessee militia. Crockett once again rose to the challenge and reenlisted with the Tennessee Mounted Gunmen on September 28, 1814. Once again, Crockett's action was greatly limited, and he returned home in December of that same year.

Davy Crockett portrait painting by S.S. (Samuel Stillman) Osgood. *National Portrait Gallery, Smithsonian Institution.*

Davy and Polly Crockett had a little more than eight years of wedded bliss that produced three children before tragedy struck with the death of Polly Crockett in March 1815. The following year, Davy married a widow with two children of her own named Elizabeth Patton, with whom he would have three more children. Not long after their marriage, Crockett contracted malaria while on a scouting trip to Alabama and was even pronounced dead by his family before miraculously recovering. In 1817, Davy Crockett entered the political realm for the first time, serving as a commissioner in Lawrence County. He was then appointed justice of the peace for the county on November 25 of that same year. On March 27, 1818, he was elected as lieutenant colonel of the Fifty-seventh Regiment of the Tennessee Militia. He served in that capacity for about one year before he resigned his positions as both the lieutenant and justice of the peace to dedicate more time to his family and other business interests.

In 1821, Crockett was elected to represent Lawrence and Hickman Counties to a seat in the Tennessee General Assembly. Crockett established himself in this role as a populist man of the people with his impassioned arguments lobbying against taxes on the poor. Probably due to his upbringing in a poor family, Crockett grew his reputation as a consistent advocate for the poverty-stricken settlers of East Tennessee. It was also during his political career that the legend of Davy Crockett the frontiersman began to grow. Crockett enjoyed the attention and notoriety of being seen as larger than life, but there was also a political angle to it, as it most assuredly aided him in his quest for office.

Crockett himself often told a story that he presented to be true about how a coonskin helped him win an election. Crockett told of being out politicking for votes in a backwoods tavern when he discovered he had no money. An expert marksman, he slipped off into the woods, where he shot and skinned a raccoon for its pelt. He brought the pelt back into the tavern, where he traded it for a round of drinks to give the crowd in an attempt to win them over. Crockett noticed that the bartender had carelessly flung the pelt under the bar with the tail sticking out from the bottom. When the bartender wasn't looking, Crockett pulled the coonskin up by the tail and used it again

Davy Crockett politicking and electioneering for votes. *Library of Congress, LC-DIG-pga-05809.*

for another round of drinks for the potential voters. He claimed the same scenario played out over and over again until he had bought the crowd ten rounds of drinks. Crockett credited the resulting good will with propelling him to victory in the election.

The same year of 1821, the Tennessee River suffered a massive flood that wiped out all of Crockett's business holdings. The setback led to the Crockett family once again going on the move, this time settling along the banks of the Obion River in Carroll County. Crockett ran for, and won, the General Assembly seat in his new county representing Carroll, Henderson, Humphreys, Madison and Perry Counties, where he continued to resonate with his constituents with his skillful demands for farmers' rights.

Crockett ran for a U.S. House of Representatives seat in the 1825 election but was defeated by Adam Rankin Alexander. Undeterred, Crockett ran against Alexander again in the 1827 election, this time successfully. Crockett and Alexander met in another rematch in 1829, with Crockett winning a second term. Crockett continued to build his populist reputation as a politician by fighting against legislation that he felt was slanted for the wealthy.

The most lasting image of Crockett the politician, however, was his courageous vote against then president Andrew Jackson's 1830 Indian Removal Act. Despite his own earlier efforts to fight against them, Davy Crockett was the only member of the Tennessee delegation to vote against this highly controversial legislation that directly led to the removal of Indians from their homelands and "resettling" them westward. These forced relocations would become known as the "Trail of Tears" for the hardships and death suffered by many of the Native Americans during this dark time of American history. Making Crockett's vote more surprising is the fact that his grandparents had been killed by Indians during a raid.

Undated engraving of Davy Crockett by Asher Brown Durand. *Wikipedia Commons.*

Crockett's vote made him very unpopular with his constituents and ended up costing him his seat in the

1831 election to William Fitzgerald. Crockett was on the losing end of the vote, but time has shown him to be on the right side of history for opposing this act. The loss would not be the end of Davy Crockett's political career, as he would reclaim the seat in 1833 before losing it once again in 1835 to Adam Huntsman. Growing weary with the political shenanigans of his opponents, upon losing the seat this time he made the now-famous proclamation, "You may all go to Hell, and I will go to Texas!"

Crockett had gotten the urge to move to Texas during his last term in Congress, and once his time in office ended, he already had a plan in place to depart to the Lone Star State. He saddled up a horse, put on his trademark coonskin cap and rode off into the proverbial sunset from Tennessee. He'd planned to become established in Texas and then send for his family to come join him, but he wouldn't live to ever see them again. A supporter of Texas independence, Crockett arrived in the state in the early part of January 1836 in the town of Nacogdoches. Crockett eventually made his way to San Antonio at the Alamo Mission on February 8, 1836.

Crockett was at the Alamo only a few weeks before a Mexican army under General Santa Anna descended on the mission on February 23. The Mexicans laid siege to the Alamo, bombarding it with artillery shells as the outnumbered American defenders returned fire. The Americans were able to fend off the initial Mexican attack, but their supplies and ammunition were dwindling rapidly. The commanding officer at the Alamo, William Barret Travis, sent for reinforcements, but his request went unanswered. As the defenders of the Alamo began to run low on gunpowder and shot, Travis decided to conserve as much as possible by letting a group of crack shots led by Crockett continue to snipe off attackers one by one.

Davy Crockett depicted in hunting gear. *Library of Congress, LC-DIG-pga-04179.*

Desperate for reinforcements, on March 3, Travis sent three men, including Davy Crockett, out of the Alamo under the cover of darkness to try to reach James Fannin, the leader of the only other group of troops in Texas, to try to persuade him to send more troops to help the defenders. Crockett and the other men joined up with another small group of forces at a creek about twenty miles from the Alamo. On the morning of March 4, some of the forces, including Crockett, were able to break back into the Alamo just before the sun came up.

The siege continued for another day before the Mexicans advanced and attacked the Americans just before sunrise on March 6 in an attempt to catch them sleeping. The defenders awoke, and a fierce battle began between the attacking Mexicans and the defending Americans. One of the few survivors of the attack, Susannah Dickinson, would later recount that Davy Crockett stopped off in the Alamo's church to say a quick prayer on his way to battle. Crockett and his men were caught exposed out in the middle of the mission before they could take cover and soon were engaged in hand-to-hand combat with the Mexicans. The defending Americans were soon overwhelmed, and the Mexican troops of Santa Anna won the Battle of the Alamo after about one and a half hours of fighting. Once fighting ceased and the Mexicans were victorious, General Santa Anna had the bodies of the dead Americans stacked up in a pile and then had wood added to the heap. He ordered the wood to be set on fire, burning the men's bodies to ashes rather than having them properly buried.

Much uncertainty and controversy surrounded the death of Davy Crockett, as it was undetermined how or when he died. Some speculation has offered that Crockett surrendered or was forcibly captured along with several other Texans only to be executed while unarmed by being hacked to death with swords. In contradiction, a witness to the battle, an American slave known only as "Joe" who was spared by the Mexicans, said that Crockett had acquitted himself well, having been found surrounded with sixteen Mexican casualties lying in his vicinity before being shot down. Another wild conspiracy theory speculates that Crockett wasn't killed at the Alamo but survived, despite being severely injured, and decided to live out the rest of his life as a farmer in Mexico. Crockett's antagonistic relationship with President Andrew Jackson was the reason given that he didn't return to the United States. It appears that Davy Crockett's death was very hard for many to accept, which led to the spread of these wild tales, not unlike conspiracy theories in the modern era.

The truth will likely never be known, but one thing is certain: Davy Crockett lived as a man of conviction and died as a man of conviction. He defended causes and people whom he felt needed an advocate, so he would have been proud to have died defending his beliefs. Crockett's legend expanded in the aftermath of the Alamo in the form of books and the Davy Crockett almanac, which published mythological exploits of this folk hero for twenty years following his death. The almanac told stories of Crockett fighting (and, of course, always defeating) bears, panthers, snakes and so on in the backwoods of Tennessee, while often sprinkling in elements of humor, as in this excerpt from the almanac:

> *I heard a loud howl behind me, that so started me that I jumped right out of water like a sturgeon. I knew it was a bear, and on turning to see how near he was, I saw a wolf but a short distance making towards me...I div down in a slantindicular direction so as to come up beyond them. When underwater an amphibious river calf saw me, and chased me to the surface. Upon breaking water they all began to chase me...upon the wolf's coming within reach, with a good blow over the nose he went off howling. The bear came on, in the most rageiferous manner...but I gave him some startling raps...And I stunned the River Calf with a blow of my club, so that he was taken. I was invited on board* [a steamboat], *but as there was ladies on board I did not like to appear in a state of nature, so I dove under the boat and swam ashore. Bears and wolves swim across the Mississippi very often.*

The legend of Davy Crockett had largely disappeared from national consciousness by the turn of the twentieth century. Crockett's life and legend got a huge boost in the 1950s from Disney when it chose him to star as a featured character for its "Frontierland" section at the Disneyland theme park. Disney also launched a television series entitled *Davy Crockett: King of the Wild Frontier*, which starred Fess Parker in the title role. The show's accompanying theme song, "The Ballad of Davy Crockett," introduced new interest into the legend and helped launch what could be described as a "Crockett Craze." The lyrics included several wild claims, such as that Crockett "killed his first bear when he was only 3" and that he "patched up the crack in the Liberty Bell." Even the opening line to the song, which proclaimed that Crockett was "born on a mountaintop," is inaccurate, as his homeplace near Limestone, Tennessee, is along a valley along the banks of the Nolichucky River. The song would come define Crockett in the minds of many and would go on to sell well over 10 million copies with versions by Bill Hayes, Fess Parker, Tennessee Ernie Ford and Mac Wiseman all reaching the top ten of various radio charts.

Spurred by the popularity of the television show and song, sales of coonskin caps skyrocketed among schoolchildren in the United States. The craze even made it all the way to Democratic vice presidential nominee Estes

An 1834 painting of Davy Crockett by John G. Chapman. *From D.W.C. Baker,* A Texas Scrap-Book *(1875).*

Kefauver, who sported a coonskin cap during his unsuccessful campaign as the running mate of Adlai Stevenson in the 1956 presidential election. The image of Crockett wearing buckskins and a coonskin cap has never been confirmed as being accurate, but it has become the standard depiction since the television series. Crockett's popularity continued to skyrocket when he was portrayed by "The Duke," John Wayne, at the height of his popularity, in a movie about the Alamo.

Coonskin cap on display at the museum located at the Davy Crockett Birthplace State Park. *Author's photo.*

The truths, half-truths and outright myths attached to Davy Crockett are so interwoven that it is extremely difficult to get an accurate picture of the man behind the legend. One thing is certain: Davy Crockett left an indelible impact on the history of East Tennessee and the United States.

Sequoyah

It is not unusual for people who have accomplished heroic feats to have other exaggerated legends and myths attached to their accomplishments. It is particularly difficult to separate fact from fiction when it comes to the Native Americans who roamed the hills of East Tennessee in the days before they possessed a written language to document their culture, with much of their history lost if not orally passed down. One of these legendary figures of Native American history is the person who first helped to create a written language for the Cherokee nation; the man, an unlikely prospect for such an accomplishment, was named Sequoyah. Fittingly, one of the most written about subjects in Cherokee Indian history has been the life and times of Sequoyah.

Painting of Sequoyah holding his Cherokee syllabary by Charles Bird King, circa 1830. *National Portrait Gallery, Smithsonian Institution.*

The exact birthdate of Sequoyah is unknown but believed to be circa 1770 in a town known to the Cherokees as Tuskegee, in the modern-day Tellico Plains area near Knoxville. Sequoyah's mother was a Cherokee named Wu-teh, said to be the niece of a Cherokee chief, while his father's exact identity is a matter of debate. Speculation of his father most often ranges from a peddler or fur trader of German or Scottish descent to other accounts stating he was what was at the time called a "half-breed" (half Indian/half white) named Nathaniel Gist (or Guess). His given birth name was George Gist (or Guess). More recently, an unverified claim has been made that Sequoyah's father was a full-blooded Cherokee, which would make Sequoyah one also. Sequoyah's father was not present in his life, which is one reason so little is known of his background. An only child, Sequoyah and his mother lived alone on a subsistence farm where he worked while his mother operated a trading post.

Sequoyah suffered an injury as a child (it is speculated that it occurred while hunting) that left him lame, which greatly hindered his physical and social development. He was then given the name Sequoyah, which loosely translates to "pig's foot" in the Cherokee language. He was blessed, however, with a great intelligence and curiosity that made him a quick learner even though he had no formal education. He had frequent interactions with white settlers and picked up skills, most notably as a silversmith. These interactions were also what sparked his interest in written language, as he spoke of their "talking leaves" that helped them communicate with one another.

He took over his mother's trading post upon her death, making it a popular draw for Cherokee men to frequent for whiskey. Sequoyah soon took to drinking in excess himself, and it began to cause issues for him with his business and in his personal life. He began to see the ramifications of his alcoholism and looked for ways to occupy his mind to break its hold on him. One of the ways he diverted his attention was by throwing himself into learning the blacksmith trade. His creations began to be sought out for their unique styles, particularly since he liked to use silver in his work. He not only successfully kicked his drinking habit but also ceased selling alcohol in his store as well.

Sequoyah began working on the Cherokee syllabary not long after this period, and he was soon preoccupied almost to the point of obsession with creating it. He neglected his crops as he pored over ideas in his quest to develop a unique Cherokee language. The idea was not immediately accepted by the Indians, as up to this point they saw written words as either a form of witchcraft or a special gift from the Great Spirit, not something that could be created by a normal man. Sequoyah's early attempts frustrated him greatly, as he couldn't conceive of an adequately simple way of conveying thoughts in a written format. Finally, he hatched an idea to create a symbol for each of the eighty-six syllables in the Cherokee language. Borrowing heavily from Latin letters he saw in a book he had in his possession, Sequoyah arbitrarily used many of these as characters to represent the Cherokee syllables. He finally created a language with which he was satisfied, but his work was far from done.

Sequoyah was quite pleased with his syllabary creation, but disappointingly, he couldn't find anyone who was willing to be taught the language. It has been said that even his wife had destroyed one of his early attempts at creating the language by burning it for fear it was inspired by evil spirits. Finally, he found the perfect student: his six-year-old daughter, Ayoka. In a scene that played out closer to a magic show than actual teaching, Sequoyah and his daughter traveled to Indian Reserves in Arkansas, where they pitched his language to the tribes there. Initially skeptical, the leaders of the Indian tribes were soon impressed with Sequoyah and his daughter's presentation. They played a "game" in which Sequoyah sent his daughter out of the room and then asked one of the other Indians to say a word, which he then wrote down on paper. He brought his daughter back into the room, and she then would say the written word aloud. Ayoka perfectly read back the words written down every time, much to the surprise and excitement of the Indian leaders.

The leaders were sufficiently impressed to allow Sequoyah to teach some of the others in their tribe for a test run. As Sequoyah went about teaching the students, rumors swirled that he was invoking evil spirits during these sessions. Once he completed their education in his system, the students displayed their understanding and grasp of the new written language for the rest of the tribe. This demonstration encouraged the rest of the western Cherokees to embrace and adopt it as their written language. Emboldened with a new confidence from this acceptance, Sequoyah headed back east to make a pitch to the Cherokees in that area. He brought with him a written copy of a speech from one of the leaders of the Arkansas Indians. Sequoyah read the speech and also won the support and embrace of the eastern Cherokees as well. In 1825, the Cherokee nation made his written work the official language, and Sequoyah was given a silver medal in his honor, which he proudly wore and displayed for the rest of his life. The Indians went on to develop their first newspaper, the *Cherokee Phoenix*, using his syllabary as the guideline.

Sequoyah went to Washington, D.C., in 1828 as an envoy to help negotiate a treaty that would become part of a planned Indian territory. While there, he met and befriended dignitaries from other Native American tribes and soon hatched an idea to create a writing system that would serve as a universal language for all Native Americans. He moved westward to Oklahoma (where he lived out the rest of his life) in 1829 and began to travel farther west into Arizona and New Mexico to pitch this new language. The Indian Removal Act had created a great rift inside the Cherokee nation between the eastern and western tribes. Being intimately familiar with both sides, Sequoyah was committed to making peace between the two tribes. A large tribal council was held on June 20, 1839, where Sequoyah spoke to members of both tribes in an attempt to broker a deal to end the hostilities. He spent the rest of his life trying to unify all the different Cherokee factions. In fact, Sequoyah died while in Mexico in August 1843 on a mission with his son Chusaleta (also known as Teesy) to locate bands of Cherokees thought to have fled south of the border during the resettlement of the Indians to the west.

Sequoyah was buried in Mexico near the border with Texas in an unknown location. Revered as a legendary hero of the Cherokees, attempts have been made through the years to conclusively locate his grave. In 1938, the Cherokee nation sent a search party to locate his grave. This initial attempt didn't lead to a conclusive find of his body, although an unidentified grave was found in the relative vicinity where he was thought to have been buried. An article was published in 2011 that claimed that a skeleton had been found in a cave in Oklahoma that had a deformed leg, lying with a few silver medals and Sequoyah's trademark pipe with a long stem. The exact whereabouts of Sequoyah's grave is still unknown and considered a great mystery to Native Americans and historians.

Sequoyah has become an icon of Native American ingenuity and perseverance. Numerous schools and other public institutions bear his name, including two mountains (one in the Great Smoky Mountains of Tennessee and one in Arkansas) and a nuclear power plant, the Tennessee Valley Authority's Sequoyah Nuclear Plant near Soddy-Daisy. It has long been said that the redwood Sequoia trees of California were named in his honor as well, but that has been called into question, as they were named by an Austrian botanist, Stephan Endlicher, who never disclosed his reasoning for the name. Despite numerous written accounts of Sequoyah's activities, much of his life and death remain shrouded in mystery. Sequoyah stands as a role model for overcoming severe physical disabilities and a lack of education to make a lasting impact on the world.

DRAGGING CANOE

The history of Native Americans is very complicated for multiple reasons, one of which is the fact that there is little surviving documentation of much of their history other than oral. Another factor stems from the inherent difficulty in placing their actions and culture in their proper context since much of their activities were diametrically opposed to the interests of white settlers moving into their territories. A clear example of this issue would be the legend of the Cherokee war chief known as Dragging Canoe, a complicated man who lived in a complicated time.

Born sometime in 1738, Dragging Canoe's father was "Little Carpenter" (Attakullakulla), one of the Cherokee leaders, and his mother was "Tamed Doe" (Nionne Ollie). Dragging Canoe contracted the smallpox disease as a young boy, which left his face severely scarred for life and became a big part of his legacy. Smallpox was often fatal to Indians in those days, so Dragging Canoe was very fortunate to survive with only that minor damage.

Wax likeness of Dragging Canoe at Sycamore Shoals State Park in Elizabethton, Tennessee. *Author's photo.*

It was also during his childhood that he earned the Dragging Canoe name, according to Cherokee legend. The story goes that like so many young boys do, Dragging Canoe wanted to prove his manhood and thus begged to be a part of a war party headed to fight the Shawnees. His father said that he could come along if he was strong enough to carry his own canoe, knowing that it would be too great a task for the youngster. Like a true warrior, Dragging Canoe would not be denied; although he couldn't carry it, he did drag it along the ground in an attempt to persuade his father to let him come. This effort earned him the Cherokee name "Tsiyu Gansini," which translates roughly to "he is dragging his canoe" in English.

Dragging Canoe saw his first real fighting action during the Anglo-Cherokee War, during which he earned a reputation for being a fierce warrior. He continued to rise in power and esteem within the Cherokee nation during the time of the American Revolution. The Cherokee Indians had cast their lot with the British as allies against the American colonial militia during the hostilities. Dragging Canoe led one of the attacks against the Americans at the Battle of Island Flats, and despite suffering a loss, he displayed courage and leadership skills that further propelled him in the resistance effort. The losses experienced by the war-weary Cherokees in these initial battles convinced Dragging Canoe's father, Little Carpenter, and another leader, "Stalking Turkey" (Oconostota), to seek a peace treaty. Dragging Canoe was defiant and refused to admit defeat, feeling that there would never be peace with the white settlers until they'd taken all the Cherokee land. He gave the following speech to the Cherokees:

> *Whole Indian Nations have melted away like snowballs in the sun before the white man's advance. They leave scarcely a name of our people except those wrongly recorded by their destroyers. Where are the Delawares?*

Artist's depiction in a period magazine of Dragging Canoe and other Cherokees negotiating a treaty with Daniel Boone and other settlers. *Internet Archive Book Images, via Wikimedia Commons.*

> *They have been reduced to a mere shadow of their former greatness. We had hoped that the white men would not be willing to travel beyond the mountains. Now that hope is gone. They have passed the mountains, and have settled upon Tsalagi ("Cherokee") land. They wish to have that usurpation sanctioned by treaty. When that is gained, the same encroaching spirit will lead them upon other land of the Tsalagi. New cessions will be asked. Finally the whole country, which the Tsalagi and their fathers have so long occupied, will be demanded, and the remnant of the Ani Yvwiya, The Real People, once so great and formidable, will be compelled to seek refuge in some distant wilderness. There they will be permitted to stay only a short while, until they again behold the advancing banners of the same greedy host. Not being able to point out any further retreat for the miserable Tsalagi, the extinction of the whole race will be proclaimed. Should we not therefore run all risks, and incur all consequences, rather than to submit to further loss of our country? Such treaties may be alright for men who are too old to hunt or fight. As for me, I have my young warriors about me. We will hold our land.*

In 1777, he led a band of Overhill Cherokees to the Chickamauga area of present-day Chattanooga. The tribe then established a settlement along South Chickamauga Creek that eventually led to them being referred to as the "Chickamauga Cherokees" by the white settlers. In 1782, the

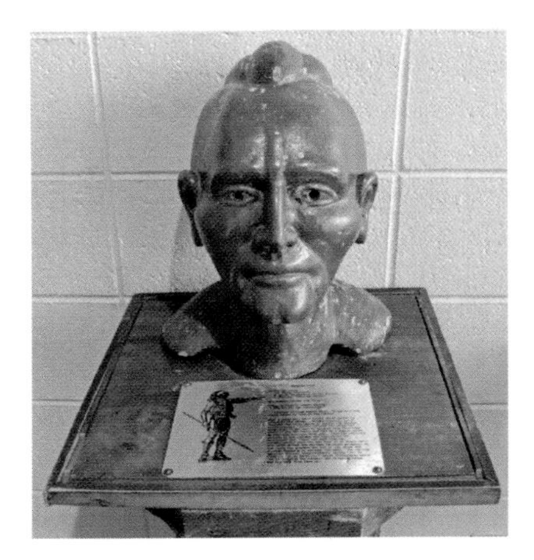

Bust of Dragging Canoe outside the museum at Sycamore Shoals State Park in Elizabethton, Tennessee. *Author's photo.*

Americans attacked the Indian settlements and forced them to move even farther south along the Tennessee River near the border with Georgia in an area that would become known as the "Five Lower Towns of the Cherokee" (Crow Town, Long Island, Lookout Mountain Town, Nickajack and Running Water).

Determined to get retribution against the encroachment of the white settlers, Dragging Canoe began to lead attacks against colonists throughout East Tennessee and on into Southwest Virginia and eastern Kentucky. Joining in these attacks with the Chickamaugas were other disaffected people from all walks of life, including mixed-blood Indians, British Loyalists, French and Spanish stragglers, thieves, murderers and other outlaws seeking to cause havoc against the colonists. Dragging Canoe and his tribe terrorized colonial settlements along the Holston, Nolichucky and Watauga Rivers. He became so notorious among white settlers that he was often credited with attacks and any other mischief that befell settlers throughout the Southeast. In many cases, those attacks were committed unbeknownst to Dragging Canoe by the renegades who had joined his tribe.

The legend of Dragging Canoe continued to grow, and he began to unify the resistance tribes of Native Americans in the Southeast. In fact, his ability to unite different tribes inadvertently led to his unusual death. On February 29 (it was a leap year), 1792, Dragging Canoe held a party back at his settlement in Chattanooga with his Chickamauga tribe to celebrate the formation of an alliance with Choctaw and Muskogee Indians. He danced all night and danced a little longer—too long, in fact, as he suffered a massive heart attack and died the next morning from the exhaustion brought about by his partying. Dragging Canoe was buried at the Running Water village near present-day Hale's Bar.

The Indian resistance movement continued to dwindle upon Dragging Canoe's death, leading to his grim prediction coming true concerning the loss of Cherokee land. These days, the legacy of Dragging Canoe is complicated—should he be considered a hero or a villain? Is he a savior or an outlaw? Should he be revered or reviled? Like many questions, the answer is a matter of perspective. He is unquestionably looked on with great pride as a hero to the Cherokees for fighting against colonial imperialism. He fought for his people with an abiding loyalty that most anyone would agree is a noble trait.

DANIEL BOONE IN EAST TENNESSEE

Daniel Boone is one of the most recognizable names in American history, famous for his exploits as a pioneer, frontiersman and explorer during the infancy of the United States. Boone blazed a trail westward known as the Wilderness Road, which cut through modern-day Cumberland Gap where the states of Kentucky, Tennessee and Virginia converge. It is estimated that during the eighteenth century, more than 200,000 migrants followed the trail Boone had created in moving westward into Kentucky and Tennessee. Daniel Boone was a restless nomad who made his mark in many different territories, including East Tennessee, during his storied lifetime. He became a folk hero in his lifetime, and his legend has only grown in the years following his death.

Born in what is now Pennsylvania, Boone began hunting at an early age, honing his skill as a marksman. His hunting and trapping talent has long been the subject of embellished folk tales wherein Boone is credited with near-superhuman bravery and skill. One such tale from his youth involves a panther that roared as it neared Boone and some other young boys out on a hunting expedition. While the other boys ran for cover, Boone is said to have stood unflinching as the panther raced toward him. The panther was set to pounce on Boone when, at the very last second, he pulled the trigger on his rifle, firing a bullet straight into the heart of the attacking animal, causing it to fall dead at his feet.

The Boone family moved to North Carolina while Daniel was young, and thereafter his schooling was sporadic at best, which led to deficiencies in his spelling ability. Boone married his neighbor, Rebecca Bryan, and looked to support his family through hunting and trapping. It was during this time that Boone first ventured into what is now East Tennessee on some of his hunting trips. Boone carried a small tomahawk-like axe on these trips and began a tradition of carving out inscriptions on various trees throughout his travels. The trees came to be known as "Boone trees"—unfortunately, this

Above: Daniel Boone protects his family. *Library of Congress, LC-USZC2-375.*

Right: Portrait of Daniel Boone. *Library of Congress, USZ62-37338.*

Road sign in Boones Creek, Tennessee, signifying the former location of one of the "Boone trees." *Author's photo.*

also led to many phony imitations springing up through the years. A beech tree was discovered to have an inscription in the Boones Creek (so named for Daniel Boone) section of Washington County, just outside Johnson City. The inscription read, "D. Boon cilled a bar on this tree in the year 1760."

The validity and authenticity of the inscription has been questioned by skeptics throughout the years, but most locals have accepted it as a valid example of one of the legitimate "Boone trees." It has been widely established that Daniel Boone camped in the area of the tree, making the legitimacy of the inscription more believable. Unfortunately, a windstorm in 1916 felled the tree, causing a crack right in the area of the inscription. Attempts to salvage the inscription failed, and no one is sure what happened to the remains.

Daniel Boone went on to explore and settle what is now known as Kentucky before eventually moving to Missouri, where he lived out his final years. Boone became famous in his lifetime in large part due to the writings of John Filson in a pamphlet entitled *The Adventures of Colonel Daniel Boon*. Intended as a work to promote Kentucky, Filson's pamphlet catapulted Daniel Boone to national prominence, making him one of the nation's first folk heroes. The stories of his exploits have grown taller through the years, and his image has changed as well. Recent depictions of Daniel Boone often show him donning a coonskin cap despite there being no evidence he ever wore one in his lifetime. Much of the image of Boone as a frontiersman today has been

Right: Portrait of Daniel Boone. *Library of Congress, LC-DIG-ppmsca-39572.*

Below: Daniel Boone protecting his daughter Jemina from Indians. *Library of Congress, LC-DIG-pga-07745.*

coopted from Davy Crockett. The main reason for this occurring is due to a popular television series in the 1950s starring Fess Parker as Boone, often shown wearing a coonskin cap. Parker had earlier starred as Davy Crockett in a similar television series and just used the same hat from that role in his new show. The popularity of the Daniel Boone television series cemented the lasting image of him in a coonskin cap despite lacking factual basis.

TIGER THE BEARHUNTER

Ordinarily, you wouldn't expect a man whose claim to fame was having killed ninety-nine black bears during hunts to be nicknamed "Tiger." James "Tiger" Whitehead, however, was no ordinary man, as his life story will reveal. The life and times of Tiger Whitehead have become an oft-told legend in his home area around Carter County, Tennessee.

James Whitehead is less well known than other mountain men such as Daniel Boone and Davy Crockett primarily because he seldom traveled far from home. He explored the woods around his home, where he became respected for his hunting prowess, as he seemed to know every nook and cranny of Carter and Unicoi Counties. Whitehead first became locally famous for being called on to hunt down and kill a dangerous tiger that had escaped from a circus that was traveling through Bristol, Tennessee. As one might expect, the thought of a semi-wild tiger running loose sent a wave of terror through the local citizenry. Being a highly skilled hunter and trapper, Whitehead had little trouble locating the tiger that had gone on the lam. He took down the tiger with one shot from his rifle, thereby earning the nickname that would stick with him for the rest of his life. Suffice it to say, there have probably been precious few hunters in East Tennessee history with a tiger kill on their résumés.

Despite the acclaim that came from this kill, Tiger Whitehead would really make his reputation from his prolific hunting of black bears. He was credited with ninety-nine kills of black bears before he died of natural causes at the ripe old age of eighty-five. One legend goes that Tiger almost lost one of those bear fights in his earlier years, as he sunk a bullet into a bear only to have it charge him—it was merely wounded and seeking to take its anger out on the rifleman. His rifle being a muzzleloader, it was quite slow and cumbersome to reload after the initial shot, so Tiger found himself in a life-threatening position. The bear stormed up to within a few feet of Tiger and then opened its mouth to let out a fierce roar. Tiger took that sliver of opportunity to shove the barrel of his rifle down the bear's throat as a diversion. He then reached into his sheath, pulled out his knife and stabbed the bear in the neck. The bear was further enraged by the stabbing but was sufficiently diverted by the rifle in its mouth to keep it occupied until it began to bleed out, eventually falling over dead. The rifle carried marks from the bear's teeth as a stark reminder of Tiger's near-death experience.

Tiger began to lose the battle with Father Time as his health started to decline, leaving him unable to participate in hunts any longer. A group of his hunting friends decided to help him get the milestone 100th kill to ensure that he hit that lofty number before he passed away. They went out and captured a bear cub and then brought it to Tiger's house to give him the can't-miss target. While he appreciated the kind gesture, Tiger refused to take the free shot. He explained to the men that he would only kill animals that were in the wild with a fair chance at escape. Sportsmanship and respect for animals of that nature were uncommon during this era, so his stance was a powerful lesson for younger hunters.

Tiger Whitehead would pass away soon after this final opportunity to make his 100th kill. His legacy lives on, as even today there are several landmarks in Carter County named in his honor, including Tiger Valley, Tiger Creek and Tiger Creek Road. Tiger's tombstone is inscribed with these words: "The Noted Hunter, James T. Whitehead, Born 1819, Died Sept. 25, 1905, (Killed 99 Bears), We Hope He Has Gone To Rest." Tiger is buried alongside his wife, Sallie Garland Chambers, who was also quite revered in Carter County for her treatment of animals. Sallie's tombstone pays homage to her own legend of raising two bear cubs and a fawn until they were able to live on their own: "She Was Not Only a Mother to the Human Race But to All Animal Kind as She Gave Nurse to One Fawn and Two Cubs. She Is Now Resting from Her Labor." Some of the stories passed down claim that Sallie literally nursed the animals from her own breast; however, that claim is doubtful, as she never bore children of her own, making the production of milk highly unlikely. It is more likely a misinterpretation of the inscription on the tombstone or an embellishment to add to the legend of how dedicated she was in her care for animals.

Many years after Tiger's death, legendary country music artist Johnny Cash came to Jonesborough to play a concert. Afterward, a friend took him to the cemetery to visit the grave of Tiger Whitehead. Cash was so impressed by the story that he wrote a song entitled "The Legend of Tiger Whitehead," describing the events of Tiger and Sally's lives, which he recorded for a children's album. For many years after Tiger's death, if someone heard an unknown gunshot in the woods, they would say, "Sounds like ol' Tiger just got his 100th bear." Tiger the bear hunter was a bird of a different feather, and that is no bull or fish tale.

SERGEANT YORK

Alvin Cullum York was born on December 13, 1887, in a log cabin in the community of Pall Mall, Tennessee. The son of a blacksmith and a homemaker, York was the third of eleven children born to William and Mary (Brooks) York. Alvin York was raised in poverty and was forced to quit school at an early age to work the family's subsistence farm. William York passed away in November 1911, leaving Alvin with the responsibility of caring for his family, as he was the oldest sibling still living in the area at the time of his father's death. York took work on the railroad and then moved into logging to provide for his mother and younger siblings. During this time, York developed a taste for alcohol and a penchant for fighting that earned him a fairly extensive arrest record.

Sergeant Alvin C. York (second from the left) poses with politicians. *Library of Congress, LC-DIG-hec-12126.*

Nothing in his early life would indicate that York would one day become one of the most decorated military heroes in American history. In fact, York himself attempted to prevent it from happening by seeking an exemption as a conscientious objector on his draft registration during World War I. Despite his aforementioned vices, York underwent a conversion experience in 1915 and became a deeply religious member of the Church of Christ in Christian Union (CCCU) who felt that killing another human was expressly forbidden in the Bible. His conscientious objector claim was denied, and his follow-up appeal of the ruling was pending when word came that he had been drafted in November 1917. York reported for duty as a private to Company G, 328th Infantry Regiment, 82nd Infantry Division, of the United States Army at Camp Gordon (now known as Fort Gordon) in Georgia.

York was still deeply conflicted about serving during wartime and met with his commanding officers to express his reservations. Major Gonzalo Edward Buxton and company commander Captain Edward Danforth were both impressed with the promise that York had shown as a soldier and respected his honest candor in expressing his beliefs. They cited scripture passages from both the Old and New Testaments that indicated sometimes the path to divine peace is brought about by the use of a sword. York was granted a ten-day leave to return to Tennessee and ponder his decision concerning his future service. They were prepared to grant York a discharge—or, at least, reassign him to a noncombat role—should he still be conflicted upon his return. Satisfied with their response and impressed with their deep knowledge of the Bible, York returned to the army after the brief break completely committed to fulfilling his duty.

After basic training, York, who had recently been promoted to the rank of corporal, and his battalion were sent to France to participate in the Meuse-Argonne Offensive. On October 8, 1918, the Americans met up with the Germans at the Decauville railway near Chatel Chéhéry. Facing heavy fire from German machine guns, the Americans suffered a large number of casualties early in the fight. Sergeant Harry Parson ordered Acting Sergeant Bernard Early, four noncommissioned officers (including York) and thirteen privates to take out the German machine guns by infiltrating the rear of the German lines. The group was initially successful in its mission and took several prisoners by taking the German headquarters by surprise. While they were tending to their new prisoners, a hail of machine gun fire rained down on the American troops from German soldiers posted across the ridge. The resulting carnage left nine American casualties (six dead and three wounded), leaving Corporal York in charge of the remaining troops.

Sergeant Alvin C. York (center). *Library of Congress, LC-DIG-npcc-00332.*

Corporal York left his men behind to guard the prisoners while he made his way across the ridge alone in an attempt to take out the German machine gunners. Facing fire from more than thirty German soldiers, York miraculously survived as he made his way up the slope, periodically calling out to the Germans to surrender while exchanging shots with them. Finally, York ran out of ammunition for his M1917 Enfield rifle, at which point he drew out his M1911 Colt .45 pistol to gun down six German soldiers (including Lieutenant Fritz Endriss) who had left a trench to charge him with their bayonets. York employed a strategy he'd learned for hunting a flock of wild turkeys while a young boy growing up in Tennessee: he knew that if he shot down the first German, the others would take cover behind the fallen man's body, making it more difficult to take the rest of them out; instead, he shot from back to front, thus enabling him to pick off the entire line one by one.

The German commanding officer, First Lieutenant Paul Jürgen Vollmer, had emptied his pistol in an attempt to stop the onrushing Corporal York. Having failed to inflict any damage and concerned for his close friend Endriss (who was lying on the ground screaming out in pain from his gunshot wound), Vollmer called out in English an offer to surrender his entire unit to York. York accepted the offer, and Vollmer blew his whistle and commanded the German troops under the command of Lieutenant Paul Adolph August Lipp to drop their weapons and surrender. The American troops rounded up the Germans, with their officers placed in front of the line. York led the contingent of German prisoners with his gun firmly planted in the back of Vollmer.

Along the way, they encountered a German platoon led by Lieutenant Karl Kübler that also laid down its weapons and surrendered at the behest of Vollmer. The growing party of prisoners was then approached by German troops led by Lieutenant Thoma, who at first refused to surrender. Corporal York pressed his gun deep into Vollmer's back to persuade him to more forcefully call for their surrender. Finally, after much debate and negotiation, Thoma agreed to surrender his troops as well, and the final prisoners were taken to march back toward the American base.

As they neared their fellow Americans in the valley, U.S. lieutenant Joseph A. Woods spotted the oncoming line, which he initially believed to be a German counterattack. Woods hastily rounded up as many soldiers as he could muster to meet the challenge before he noticed that the German soldiers were unarmed. As the line of prisoners approached, York called out, "Corporal York reports with prisoners, sir." When Lieutenant Woods asked York how many prisoners, he replied, "Honest, Lieutenant, I don't know." The eventual headcount revealed that Corporal York and the 7 Americans brought back an amazing total of 132 prisoners in all, including 4 officers among them. Whether it was for reasons of pride or if he simply couldn't comprehend what had happened, Vollmer vehemently denied that York was able to accomplish his feats alone. He went to his grave saying the happenings were the work of a much larger operation by the Americans forces.

Alvin York was promoted to sergeant for his heroics, and a host of other awards flooded in, including the United States Medal of Honor, World War I Victory Medal and the Distinguished Service Cross. The French awarded him the Croix de Guerre and Legion of Honor, and Italy awarded him the Croce di Guerra al Merito. In all, York received close to fifty medals for his valor. Despite these honors, the story of Sergeant York's accomplishments

Sergeant Alvin C. York. *Library of Congress, LC-DIG-ggbain-29128.*

was largely unknown back home in the United States. It stayed untold until journalist George Patullo wrote an article for the April 26, 1919 edition of the *Saturday Evening Post* that detailed the amazing feats of York's bravery. The story of the religious patriot from deep in the hills of Tennessee captivated the nation and made York an icon of the American soldier. York was soon brought in on furlough to tour New York City and Washington, D.C., where grand celebrations were held in his honor.

Within a week of being discharged from service, Alvin York married Gracie Loretta Williams back home in Pall Mall. York received numerous offers to profit from his fame in the form of endorsements and personal appearances and by selling the rights to his life story. He politely declined them, as he was more inclined to lend his name to charitable causes and organizations. His postwar activities included a passionate plea for assistance to his rural community in the form of improved road service. He also began the Alvin C. York Foundation to bring an increased focus on educational opportunities for young people in his home area of Tennessee.

Ever the patriot, York attempted to reenlist in the army at the outbreak of World War II despite being fifty-four years old and fighting myriad health issues, including being overweight, showing signs of being in the early stages of diabetes and having crippling arthritis. He was denied in this effort; however, he was commissioned to be a major in the U.S. Army Signal Corps. In this role, York helped raise money during bond drives and for the Red Cross and also toured training facilities, where he inspired young troops with his inspirational stories.

Having long rebuffed attempts to make his life into a movie, York eventually relented reluctantly when he was seeking to gain funds

Alvin York giving a speech to military recruits in Camp Claiborne, Louisiana, on May 7, 1942. *Library of Congress.*

to establish a Bible school. In 1941, a motion picture about his life entitled *Sergeant York* was finally made. The film, starring the legendary Gary Cooper in the title role, was a smash hit and earned eleven Oscar nominations (winning two, including the Academy Award for Best Actor to Cooper for his portrayal of York), going on to become the highest-grossing film of 1941.

Alvin York would see his health problems escalate and suffered a debilitating stroke in 1948. Additional strokes and complications ultimately kept him bedridden from 1954 until his death on September 2, 1964, of a cerebral hemorrhage at the age of seventy-six. York was buried at the Wolf River Cemetery in Pall Mall, leaving behind his wife and seven surviving children (a son, Sam Houston York, died in infancy) to mourn. York left behind a legacy filled with patriotism, honor, family, service and faith that is still remembered to this day. Seven public buildings and many other public monuments have been erected in his honor. Not a bad life's work for a poor hillbilly from the mountains of Tennessee.

Part II
Legendary Events in East Tennessee History

The (Almost) Deadly Duel Between the President and the Governor

Modern politics are often perceived to get nasty, with politicians routinely engaging in mudslinging and negative campaigning. These days, the worst outcome of these campaigns normally is bruised egos and hard feelings. People tend to think of earlier politicians as being more civil and gentlemanly in their discourse; however, a quick study of the history books paints an entirely different portrait of our early political process. The most commonly known example of political rivalries is the duel between two government officials considered to be among the Founding Fathers of the United States, Alexander Hamilton and Aaron Burr, which resulted in Hamilton's death from a gunshot wound in 1804. A similar duel was narrowly averted between future president of the United States Andrew "Old Hickory" Jackson and the governor of Tennessee, John "Nolichucky Jack" Sevier.

The events leading up to the escalation of tensions between Jackson and Sevier are thought to have begun with Jackson seeking the position of major general of the Tennessee state militia. Then governor Sevier favored another candidate, George Conway, for the position and aided Conway in securing it. This interference enraged Jackson, and when word got back to Sevier of his anger, Sevier was quoted as describing Jackson as a "poor, pitiful, pettifogging lawyer."

Andrew Jackson, the seventh president of the United States. *National Portrait Gallery, Smithsonian Institution.*

Once his term as governor came to an end and he was prevented from running for reelection for two years due to term limits, John Sevier sought to secure the same position he had denied Jackson as major general of the militia. This time, however, Jackson turned the tables on Sevier by securing the position with the help of the new governor, Archibald Roane. After waiting out his mandatory two years, a motivated Sevier ran for the governorship again. During the election campaign cycle, Andrew Jackson stepped forward with paperwork alleging that Sevier had engaged in a major fraud scheme in which he allegedly swindled landownership by using forged records to secure large parcels for his own possession. Furthermore, Jackson claimed that Sevier had engaged in bribery to help in covering up the fraud. Despite the scandalous allegations, Sevier went on to win the governorship, but his tensions with Jackson soon began to boil over in the aftermath.

A confrontation between the two men occurred on October 1, 1803, in the courthouse square of Knoxville, Tennessee. An eyewitness account of the altercation described a scene in which emotions escalated and heated words were exchanged between the rivals. Sevier is claimed to have challenged Jackson to a swordfight to settle their differences. Jackson was forced to decline, as he carried only a cane and not a sword. Sevier continued to badger Jackson and belittled his lack of military service prior to becoming a major general. Jackson gave a spirited defense of his service, to which Sevier allegedly replied, "I know of no great service you rendered the country, except taking a trip to Natchez with another man's wife." The snide remark brought up the controversial beginning of Jackson's relationship with his wife, Rachel. Prior to moving back to Tennessee, Rachel Jackson had been married to a man named Lewis Robards while living in Harrodsburg, Kentucky. While still in Kentucky, Rachel had separated from Robards and assumed that he had sought out, and been granted, a divorce. Rachel met Andrew Jackson in Tennessee, and the two were quite smitten with each other from the onset. Andrew and Rachel proceeded to get married before discovering that the divorce with Robards had never been finalized. The incident became a very sensitive and embarrassing episode for Jackson, and he had no intention of letting Sevier get away with the insult. Jackson lunged at Sevier, and onlookers had to separate the two before things spiraled completely out of control.

Still enraged, the following day Jackson wrote a letter to Sevier that ended with a challenge for the men to meet up to duel with pistols. Jackson wrote, "My friend who will hand you this will point out the time and place when and where I shall expect to see you with your friend and no other person. My friend and myself will be armed with pistols. You cannot mistake me or my meaning." Sevier responded with a sarcastic reply that read in part, "I shall wait on you with pleasure at any time and place not within the State of Tennessee, attended by my friend with pistols, presuming you know nothing about the use of any other arms. Georgia, Virginia and North Carolina are all within our vicinity. You cannot mistake me or my meaning."

Several more letters were exchanged in the following days culminating in a meeting between the men for a duel on October 16, 1803. The true story of what happened that day will likely never be known, as this is where the story gets murky. Accounts of what took place would make modern-day political "spin doctors" look fair and balanced by comparison. A witness for Jackson claimed that Jackson met up with Sevier on horseback; Sevier then dismounted his horse and drew his pistols on Jackson, causing "Old Hickory" to do likewise. At this point, it is claimed that Sevier ran and hid behind a tree in fear for his life. Despite pleas and goading from Jackson, Sevier was described as hiding cowardly behind the tree. Finally, Jackson was said to have been persuaded to cease once it became obvious that Sevier had no intention of engaging.

Unsurprisingly, defenders of Sevier told a completely different version of how events unfolded. An anonymous letter published in the November 25, 1803 edition of the *Tennessee Gazette* claimed that the reason Sevier was unable to engage in the duel was the result of Sevier's horse (on which his firearms were stationed in their holster) being spooked off in the mêlée. The letter went on to suggest that Sevier couldn't have engaged without the missing pistols and hid behind the tree due to being unarmed. Later, Sevier apologists would offer up various other explanations for Sevier's actions (or lack thereof). Sevier was frequently cast in these accounts as a gentleman and statesman who diffused the situation with diplomacy and reason versus the hotheaded Jackson.

The version of events one chose to believe tended to depend on which side of the political spectrum one was on. John Sevier was wildly popular in East Tennessee due to his heroics during the Revolutionary War, while Andrew Jackson would go on to become a hero during the War of 1812, which propelled him into the White House. The proposed duel with John Sevier wasn't the only time Jackson was involved in a duel. A few years after his confrontation with Sevier, Jackson met another attorney named Charles Dickinson in a duel. Jackson killed Dickinson in the ensuing gunfight, while he himself was almost killed by a bullet that became lodged near his heart.

Fortunately, the duel between Andrew Jackson and John Sevier didn't take place, as it would potentially have led to the demise of one of the most beloved governors in Tennessee's history or the death of the man who would become the seventh president of the United States. The smear campaigns and television ads that are hallmarks of modern politics seem rather tame in comparison.

THE TRAGIC TALE OF MURDEROUS MARY THE ELEPHANT

One of the most unusual events in East Tennessee history happened in 1916 and involved the public hanging of a circus elephant now known as "Murderous Mary" in the town of Erwin, Tennessee. It is an incident that has been the subject of much discussion, debate, disagreement and disgust for decades. The full details of what transpired are quite murky, as the retelling of the story has added different layers and sensationalized details to the legend.

Mary, advertised as weighing more than five tons and being the largest living land animal on earth, was a major draw as part of a traveling circus known as "Sparks World Famous Shows." The show traveled from Jenkins, Kentucky, to St. Paul, Virginia, as part of its normal circuit. Due to the sudden departure of Mary's regular trainer, the owner of the circus, Charlie Sparks, was forced to quickly shuffle his staff and hire an inexperienced assistant keeper, Walter "Red" Eldridge, to help care for Mary. Eldridge, a drifter who was originally from Indiana, had previously been employed as a janitor and bellman at the Riverside Hotel in St. Paul. Eldridge had neither experience as a zookeeper nor any experience working directly with elephants prior to his hiring. The only qualities he brought to the table were the desire to work in the circus business and a willingness to learn.

The circus traveled from St. Paul on to Kingsport, Tennessee, by railroad car, and this is where things went sour. The morning show in Kingsport went well and drew a large, enthusiastic crowd. Afterward, the elephants and other animals were scheduled to be taken to a pond just down the street to cool off, get a drink and relax before the night show. On the way to the watering hole, Mary spotted a piece of watermelon rind and attempted to reach it with her trunk when the woefully inexperienced Red Eldridge used his bull hook to block her. Mary shook her head and snorted at this first use of the bull hook, but determinedly, she once again reached out for the rind. Eldridge, overreacting perhaps due to embarrassment at his inability to control the elephant in front of the crowd that by this time had gathered to watch, whacked Mary even harder with the bull hook. The blow caught Mary on the side of the head, touching off the tragic set of events that are talked about to this day. Mary, having been accustomed to more delicate handling by previous keepers, became enraged and grabbed the stunned Eldridge with her trunk, threw him into a drink stand and then proceeded to stomp on his head until it exploded in a horrific display of brutality.

The shocked and terrified onlookers began to frantically scramble for safety for fear of a rampage. Once it became obvious that Mary had calmed down, the crowd began to gather back around (at a safe distance), whereupon people began to scream, "Kill the elephant!" A local blacksmith who was working at his shop, Hench Cox, heard the commotion and drew his pistol, which he then fired at Mary in an attempt to take her down. He shot five rounds into the elephant to no avail, as her thick skin prevented the bullets from penetrating. The chaos continued as circus owner Charlie Sparks arrived at the scene and addressed the crowd, but the damage had already been done. The crowd became even more vocal as it turned into a lynch mob thirsty for vengeance against the murdering beast.

The county sheriff came and took Mary to the local courthouse, where she was "arrested" and kept until her punishment was decided. Public outcry for her execution continued to grow during this time as the stories of the attack spread with embellishment. The media added to the sensationalism with reports of Mary impaling Red Eldridge with her tusk (despite the fact that she didn't have tusks) and menacingly hurling his body at the crowd of onlookers. Local officials huddled to determine the next course of action to pacify the growing sentiment from the throngs of people seeking vengeance.

Initially, Charlie Sparks lobbied for mercy, as Mary had been a longtime performer in his show without prior incident. Being the businessman that he was, Sparks also fretted over losing a high-priced asset, as elephants routinely fetched in the vicinity of $8,000—a huge amount of money in those days.

Sparks relented once he finally determined that the public pressure was too great to overcome. Upcoming show dates were canceled once news of the tragedy spread, as no one wanted to deal with a murdering elephant in their town. Rumors even swirled that a vigilante mob was gathering with an old cannon from the Civil War to take justice into its own hands.

The decision was ultimately made that Mary had to be destroyed; however, there were few options of carrying out the execution due to her size after the earlier attempt to shoot her had proved futile. Oddly enough, a similar elephant execution occurred in 1903, when a rogue elephant named Topsy was electrocuted at Coney Island in New York for killing a spectator. Kingsport officials determined that they didn't have the level of electricity necessary to perform an electrocution in this case. After much debate and discussion, the decided method of execution was to have her transported to the nearby town of Erwin, Tennessee, in Unicoi County, where they would hang her from a railroad crane in public view to appease the mob clamoring for her death.

A reported crowd of three thousand, including children, gathered for the spectacle on the cold, rainy afternoon of September 13, 1916, at the Clinchfield Railroad Yard. There has long been speculation and rumors that Charlie Sparks, ever the businessman, saw this public display as an opportunity to make a few sales of food and other merchandise. In reality, it is highly unlikely that Sparks used this spectacle as a marketing ploy, as the circus had performed a show (sans Mary) in Erwin just prior to the hanging and hadn't promoted or sold tickets for the hanging. Word of mouth had traveled around the area, and by all accounts, the massive crowd that gathered had caught the railroad and the circus performers by surprise. Public hangings of human criminals weren't entirely uncommon during this era, so the hanging of an elephant would have drawn much interest and morbid curiosity.

Finally, the first attempt at hanging Mary was initiated by chaining her legs and then draping another chain over her neck before lifting the massive animal up with a winch on the one-hundred-ton railroad derrick crane. The first chain slowly lifted Mary off the ground as she struggled and kicked to free herself. Suddenly the chain snapped under the pressure of the elephant's weight, causing Mary to violently crash down on the ground. She wasn't

The former Clinchfield Railroad railyard at Erwin where "Murderous Mary" the elephant is supposed to be buried in an unmarked grave. *Author's photo.*

dead but had suffered severe injuries, including a broken hip in the fall. Her injuries caused her to cry out in pain and twist her body in a vain attempt to get back off the ground. Hearing her cries and seeing that she was free from the chain, many onlookers fled in terror, thinking that they were about to become victims of a rampaging elephant. Her injuries were too severe for Mary to rise off the ground under her own power, so officials quickly moved to make a second attempt to finish the execution using a heavier chain.

The second attempt succeeded in lifting her off the ground by the neck, and due to her injuries, Mary was unable to give much of a struggle this time. Within minutes, Mary was dead, and her lifeless body hung motionless from the derrick crane on full display for the gathered crowd of onlookers. The execution of Mary had finally satisfied the bloodthirsty mob, which had sought her death as payback for smashing the head of Red Eldridge. After several more minutes, Mary was slowly lowered to the ground, where her body was inspected by a veterinarian prior to her burial. The veterinarian discovered an infected tooth near the point where Red Eldridge had struck her with the bull hook, which may explain her uncharacteristically violent reaction to the blow. Mary was eventually buried near the site of her death in an unmarked grave in an attempt to make the whole incident go away.

Sparks World Famous Shows packed up and moved on to the next town, minus one elephant, a fact that didn't go unnoticed by the other elephants in the show, which took time to adjust to the mysterious loss of their leader. Elephants are highly intelligent and sensitive animals that are very perceptive of their surroundings, so they sensed that something was amiss. Eventually, the elephants and Sparks World Famous Shows returned to normal as memory of the incident slowly faded. The show must go on, as they say.

Unfortunately, this incident is still today a source of great controversy and dispute locally, with many of the actual facts remaining cloudy. Close to a century later, the hanging of "Murderous Mary" remains a cautionary tale of the sensitive balance between humans and creatures of the wild.

THE SECRET CITY OF OAK RIDGE

A place with the nickname "Secret City" just has to be full of legendary stories, and Oak Ridge lives up to that promise. Before it became the city it is today, the land that makes up Oak Ridge consisted of sparsely populated rural farming communities scattered throughout the area. These farms had been passed down through families who had worked the land for generations in the sleepy locality that rests just twenty-five miles west of Knoxville. Little did anyone (save for one man) know that this area would one day become home to one of the most scientifically sophisticated operations in the world—one that would help bring an end to World War II.

World War II was in full swing in 1942 when an idea was hatched that would be given the codename of the "Manhattan Project." The backstory leading up to the Manhattan Project begins with the Japanese surprise bombing of Pearl Harbor on December 7, 1941. Pearl Harbor gave a sense of urgency to the United States to develop the idea of atomic weapons. The idea of nuclear fission had been discovered by German chemist Otto Hahn and his assistant, Fritz Strassmann, on December 17, 1938. This discovery led to a sense of panic that the Germans were developing their own atomic weapon, and this created an arms race to see who could first use this knowledge to develop the idea into a working bomb. The Manhattan Project was America's effort to win this race, and time was of the essence.

United States major general Leslie Groves was placed in charge of the project, and he wasted no time in heading to Tennessee to scope out the feasibility of using the land for a facility in this development. Groves was

Road marker reflecting the original location of the Scarboro community. *Brian Stansberry, via Wikimedia Commons.*

Aerial photo of Oak Ridge. Tennessee. *Energy.gov (HD.30.003), via Wikimedia Commons.*

Aerial view of the facilities of Oak Ridge, Tennessee. *Energy.gov (HD.30.331.), via Wikimedia Commons.*

impressed with the area, as it had several things making it ideal: it was sparsely populated, land was cheap and perfectly laid out, the area was accessible and utilities were sufficient coming from the Norris Dam. President Franklin D. Roosevelt issued a presidential proclamation that essentially laid claim to the land by eminent domain. A civil action letter was delivered to homeowners notifying them they were being displaced to create the "Kingston Demolition Range"; they were told to vacate their premises immediately. Not surprisingly, this order didn't go over well with those affected, and they attempted to fight the order both in court and by protest, to no avail.

Construction began on the massive plant and accompanying housing that would become a key component of the Manhattan Project. Trailer houses and hutments (tiny sixteen- by sixteen-foot one-room shacks) were brought in a residential section that would be named Happy Valley. The newly built town needed a name, and after receiving many employee suggestions, the name Oak Ridge was chosen primarily due to its tame, rural sound, which wouldn't draw unnecessary attention. The government represented the facility as the "Clinton Engineer Works," or CEW, an innocuous-sounding name that belied the true nature of work conducted there. Employees were issued security badges and strongly urged to keep their work tasks a secret. The locally hired employees at the plant initially had no idea that the true nature of their work was to produce enriched uranium for use in atomic weapons. While not fully understanding their mission, employees began to realize the important nature of their work, as they were subjected to lie detector screening and made to sign a security declaration informing them of potential consequences for revealing any secrets under the Espionage Act of 1917.

On July 25, 1945, a shipment of uranium-235 left the Oak Ridge Y-12 facility headed for the island of Tinian, where it was used in the atomic bomb nicknamed "Little Boy." On August 6, President Harry S Truman authorized the dropping of the Little Boy bomb on the Japanese city of Hiroshima, killing more than 20,000 Japanese soldiers, with an estimated 70,000 to 146,000 more civilian casualties. The news of the bomb dropping touched off a raucous celebration in Oak Ridge among

Aerial view of housing at Oak Ridge, Tennessee. *Energy.gov (HD.30.331.), via Wikimedia Commons.*

Left: WACs marching at Oak Ridge. *Energy.gov (HD.30.404.), via Wikimedia Commons.*

Below: Calutron operators working at their panels in the Y-12 plant at Oak Ridge, Tennessee, during World War II. The calutrons were used to refine uranium ore into fissile material.

the workers at the nuclear facilities. Many of them still didn't have a full grasp on exactly how their work had directly played a hand in building the bomb, as security had been so tight that employees weren't allowed to discuss their individual job responsibilities with one another. The bombing of Hiroshima and then Nagasaki on August 9 directly led to

Atomic cloud over Hiroshima, taken from *Enola Gay* flying over Matsuyama, Shikoku. *509th Operations Group, via Wikimedia Commons.*

Japan's surrender, thus ending World War II. The postwar period led to a slow transition of Oak Ridge from the "Secret City" to a more normal existence.

Long before the area around Oak Ridge became Oak Ridge, there was a local man named John Hendrix who died twenty-eight years before the building of the nuclear facilities. Hendrix was quite an eccentric local character in the area, as he was prone to wandering off by himself into the woods for days on end. He was convinced that he possessed divine skills of prophecy for seeing the future, which was reinforced when he correctly predicted that a railroad was coming from Knoxville into Anderson County. He also correctly predicted that a local barn would burn to the ground, which ended up taking place exactly as he had described. Many townspeople began to believe John Hendrix to be in possession of some unique divine gift.

After a particularly lengthy stay of forty nights in the woods, Hendrix claimed that a voice told him he would be able to see visions of the future. Once he returned to town, he passionately began to spread the word of the things revealed to him in his dreams while in the woods. He spoke of "great

A celebration of the surrender of Japan. *Ed Westcott, U.S. Army, Manhattan Engineer District, via Wikimedia Commons.*

buildings and factories that will help to win the greatest war that will ever be" and then spoke of "thousands of people running to and fro" as the earth shook from the building of new massive facilities. Hendrix even went so far as to name specific townspeople who would be alive to see the events unfold.

John Hendrix was viewed as a quack by most of his peers in the time he lived, yet time proved that virtually every detail he spelled out came true. Hendrix died in 1915 at the age of forty-nine of complication from tuberculosis. The fulfillment of his prophecy concerning Oak Ridge earned him the posthumous nickname the "Prophet of Oak Ridge." Was his prophecy mysticism or madness? Did Hendrix have a connection with the future or a disconnection from reality? The story of John Hendrix leaves many more questions than answers.

Part III
Moonshining in the Mountains

The Background of Moonshining in East Tennessee

The typical idea of the Appalachian moonshiner evokes images of a simple backwoods farmer whipping up a small batch of 'shine, mountain dew or corn squeezins in a little still at the back of his barn to drink from a little brown jug. Like many stereotypes, there's a large element of truth to that picture these days, but there was a time when moonshining was big business in East Tennessee. In fact, organized crime syndicates involving entire families weren't uncommon in which various family members held different job roles in their "Hillbilly Mafia."

The days of Prohibition along with the hard times that accompanied the onset of the Great Depression were a potent combination that led many an Appalachian to run afoul of the law by dealing in illicit whiskey. The ready availability of all the ingredients and equipment needed to make the potent homebrew was too much temptation for many poor mountaineers to pass up. The lure of potential big money and widespread disdain of the federal government telling them how to conduct their lives led many locals to defy the law. As more and more money came into play, the moonshine operations took on the look of a normal business with multiple employees. There were the brewers who made the 'shine and the bootleggers who would distribute the finished product in the back of cars souped up to outrun the law.

Tennessee moonshine barrel. *Author's photo.*

As is often the case, the more the money potential grew, the more aggressively the moonshiners would expand and defend their operations. During this era, many moonshiners earned a bad reputation for intimidation and threatening anyone who got in the way of their "business," whereas before this period most local citizens were either indifferent to or even protective of the moonshiners. The boom in wealth from the liquor trade led to competition and, in some cases, violence between rival moonshining families. Often, someone in one of the competing families would inform on his competitors in the hopes of having them put out of business by the government, thereby giving him a local monopoly.

Any time there is a substantial amount of illegal money to be made, it attracts the fringes of society, bringing shady characters with checkered pasts out of the woodwork. Inevitably, the moonshining trade brought thieves, liars and other undesirables to the industry. A sense of lawlessness swept through many rural communities, which were ill-prepared to combat the new challenges brought to their sleepy towns. The local police had their hands full trying to break up the moonshine operations, which continued to thrive until the end of the Great Depression. Many stories, myths and legends of the moonshining industry from this era have

A "lil brown jug" used to carry moonshine. *Author's photo.*

been passed down through the generations. It is difficult to distinguish fact from fiction, as most of the events weren't documented, aside from the occasional newspaper story, which isn't surprising for an industry dependent on operating in the shadows.

East Tennessee has long been a hotbed of moonshining activity, and that history has made its way into numerous songs, stories, movies and pop culture. The little community of Cosby in Cocke County was once hailed as the "Moonshine Capital of the World" for its prolific production during the first half of the twentieth century. Cosby was a major point of origin for illegal liquor making its way into the larger markets of Knoxville and Oak Ridge. Cocke County was also home to the late Marvin "Popcorn" Sutton, who earned infamy in recent years after his appearance in a documentary entitled *This Is the Last Dam Run of Likker I'll Ever Make*, describing his moonshine production methods in Maggie Valley, North Carolina. Other references to the moonshining profession include the song "Copperhead Road" by Steve Earle and the motion picture (with accompanying movie theme ballad) entitled *Thunder Road* starring Robert Mitchum.

THUNDER ROAD

"Thunder Road" was the real code name given by the feds to an overall operation to shut down moonshiners and bootlegging ridge-runners in the Appalachian Mountains. Locals used the term to refer to a route that originated in Harlan County, Kentucky, and then made its way through Claiborne and Union Counties in Tennessee on into the city of Knoxville. In his research for writing the screenplay to *Thunder Road*, Robert Mitchum combed through numerous records of actual events from the federal agency known as the Alcohol Tax Unit (ATU) and spoke with revenuers about their tales involving Appalachian moonshiners. Mitchum then used this research to piece together a storyline that would become the finished movie.

The resulting movie and theme song (aptly named "The Ballad of Thunder Road") tell the story of the fictional character Lucas "Luke" Doolin, a Korean War veteran and farmer from Harlan, Kentucky, who turned into a midnight bootlegger driving down the backroads delivering corn liquor into Knoxville. Mitchum cast himself in the starring role of Doolin and wrote a part specifically for Elvis Presley that would have had him co-starring as Doolin's younger brother. Elvis was excited about the prospect of being in the film, but his notoriously difficult manager, Colonel Tom Parker, blew the deal with an outrageously high salary demand that was more than the entire film budget.

The song ends with Luke Doolin speeding through the Knoxville areas of Kingston Pike headed into Bearden, where he meets his demise in a sensational fiery car crash while running from the law at a speed of ninety miles per hour. The film version has the crash taking place in Memphis, which is quite a stretch, as it is about five hundred miles from Harlan to Memphis—quite a long journey for a load of moonshine. Presumably, this ending was written when the prospect of Elvis Presley (a resident of Memphis) appearing in the movie was still deemed likely.

The movie and song were wildly popular throughout Appalachia and especially so in East Tennessee, where the film would play in local drive-in theaters for decades after its release. Fans of the movie speculated as to whom, if anyone, the movie was actually based on. For his part, Mitchum neither confirmed nor denied that the film was based on a particular individual. Fans of the tale combed through local records of car crashes at the time stated in the song and movie, to no avail. Was Luke Doolin's story completely made up? If not, who was it who met his doom trying to evade the police? Most people concluded that the details were too specific to have been completely fabricated—meaning that it had to have been at least loosely based on a true story. The problem then became that so many different true stories matched up that people from all over were convinced they knew the "real" story.

The truth has never been fully revealed; however, the field has been narrowed to the point that there is a general consensus as to the likely primary backstory. It should come as no surprise that the prime candidate hailed from the aforementioned "Moonshine Capital of the World," Cosby in Cocke County: one Rufus "Rufe" Gunter. Gunter was quite famous locally for his exploits as a stock car racer, a skill that was honed from his time running moonshine down the backroads. In fact, many of the original NASCAR racers got their start from bootlegging whiskey; the sport of dirt track racing was born directly from the industry. Rufus Gunter lived a hardscrabble life very similar to Mitchum's character of Lucas Doolin and, tragically, died a somewhat similar death in a car crash in January 1953. Rather than a fiery crash, Gunter died when his car ran off a bridge into the Holston River in Knox County during a high-speed chase with revenuers in hot pursuit. Gunter was thirty-three at the time of his death, which would have approximated the age of Mitchum's character in the film.

While the true story may never be known, Rufus Gunter is the person most commonly linked as the main source of material for the movie. The legend of Thunder Road lives on in amusement park rides and in the names of a local distillery. The life of local bootleggers was filled with excitement, danger and, occasionally, death, which is why the world is still fascinated by their stories.

COPPERHEAD ROAD

The song "Copperhead Road" is loosely based on a real road near Mountain City in Johnson County, Tennessee. Mountain City is a picturesque rural backdrop that would rival anything seen in a Norman Rockwell painting, with its gently rolling hills and peaceful meadows surrounded by majestic mountains. The song describes a mythical third-generation descendant of the area named John Lee Pettimore III, whose father and grandfather had previously engaged in the moonshining and bootlegging trades. Upon his discharge from the army following the Vietnam War, the younger Pettimore

A view of the road leading into Copperhead "Hollow" Road. *Author's photo.*

A mailbox still lists the address as Copperhead Road. *Author's photo.*

The road sign atop of this stop sign has been removed, reflecting the ongoing popularity despite the name change to Copperhead Hollow Road. *Author's photo.*

hatches a plan to forego moonshining in favor of growing the newer cash crop: marijuana.

The real Copperhead Road is in a remote part of the county and has long had a reputation for questionable activities, which made it a locally infamous place well before the song's release. The popularity of the song, combined with the reverence and respect some people bestow on moonshiners and outlaws, made Copperhead Road a popular destination for another illegal activity: the stealing of road signs. These thefts were so prevalent that the local officials decided they needed to change the name to "Copperhead Hollow Road" in an attempt to end this pilfering of signs. The change in names did little to slow down the theft of the road signs, as they are still frequently missing, which can lead an unwitting driver to pass right by the turnoff.

JOHNSON CITY: "LITTLE CHICAGO OF THE SOUTH"

Johnson City is a bustling college town in the corner of East Tennessee and home to a thriving downtown business district. In fact, Johnson City is currently a model for the surrounding area, as it has commercial and residential development that would be the envy of virtually any Appalachian city. The present narrative belies a much darker past, as Johnson City was once a hotbed for illegal activity when bootlegging, gambling and prostitution were rampant vices that had a chokehold on the downtown area during Prohibition. The seedy reputation for criminal activity and political corruption earned Johnson City the unflattering moniker of "Little

Chicago" in a disparaging comparison to the city of Chicago, Illinois, which was riddled with organized crime at the time.

In the early part of the twentieth century, Johnson City served as a crossroad for the railroads, making it a frequent stopover for travelers passing through the area. Centrally located in between Chicago and Miami, Florida, it isn't farfetched to think of Johnson City as a natural hub along the crime highway. Much speculation and rumors have centered on three primary buildings: one known as the Montrose Court Apartment complex; another being the John Sevier Hotel; and, lastly, the Windsor Hotel. A local newspaper, the *Johnson City Staff News*, reported in its April 7, 1929 issue of a major raid by federal, state and local officers on numerous speakeasies in Johnson City. The raid uncovered large quantities of homebrew, as the officers had broken 945 bottles in all by the end of the shakedown.

The well-documented penchant for lawbreaking activity has fueled much speculation that a group in Johnson City was affiliated with the Chicago crime syndicate, whether loosely or on a more official basis. The most sensational legend is that notorious mob boss Al Capone, who held the dubious distinction of being "Public Enemy No. 1," had a local headquarters in Johnson City. A highly secretive man who traveled using aliases, Capone did not own any property in his real name, nor did he even have a deposit account with a bank, so tracking his involvement in any Johnson City holdings would be nearly impossible. Capone was heavily involved in bootlegging during Prohibition, where he made his fortune with a violent reign as the head of the Chicago Outfit. As he became increasingly more paranoid, Capone tried to stay away from Chicago as much as possible by traveling via railroad to destinations all over the southeastern part of the United States to visit his regional "businesses."

The stories of Al Capone's affiliation with Johnson City stem in part from the lawless reputation and the elaborate infrastructure around the city. There were said to be intricate underground passageway routes in the downtown area, making it plausible that they could have been used for escapes from shakedowns. Hidden doors have been found in several of the former speakeasies in recent years, adding credence to their use by organized crime. Political corruption ran amok in Johnson City during the days of Prohibition, with numerous allegations of police misconduct during that time. Organized crime bosses tend to not keep diaries, so most of the evidence of Capone's presence in the city is circumstantial, with the oral legends passed down through the generations being the only cited proof.

"Public Enemy No. 1" Al Capone, head of the Chicago Syndicate. *Chicago Bureau (Federal Bureau of Investigation), via Wikimedia Commons.*

Despite the lack of concrete proof, it is difficult to comprehend why Capone would *not* have used Johnson City as a hub. Johnson City was a lawless city right in the middle of the trip to some of Capone's favorite destinations, Miami and West Palm Beach, Florida. Bootlegging had a strong chokehold on the area around Johnson City at the time of the late 1920s, which was right in the middle of Capone's reign of terror. Capone was well known to visit the headquarters of his regional operations to ensure that they felt his presence while allowing him to personally broker deals for running the liquor. The most prevalent story is that Capone used the apartment house at Montrose Court as his local headquarters. First built in 1922, the apartment at Montrose Court was quite majestic for its time, making it a suitable locale for a traveling mob boss. Stories have circulated for years that Capone engaged in a poker match at Montrose Court on at least one occasion. Regardless of whether Capone really did make Johnson City a regular stop, it is highly likely that some of his henchmen were regulars who would have been drawn to the area to retrieve some of the large quantities of moonshine to be found.

For all the talk about organized crime's influence in Johnson City, precious few prominent local people have been willing to go on record about the alleged organized crime operations to this day. Numerous stories have passed down from prior generations, but there appears to be either honor among thieves or, perhaps, a lingering healthy fear of retribution for being a snitch even this many years later. The sordid reputation of Johnson City lasted well past the Prohibition era, as the city was named one of the twenty-five cities in the United States to be a "hotbed of vice conditions" in the February 26,

Present-day Montrose Court, widely rumored to be Al Capone's hangout in Johnson City. *Author's photo.*

"Capone's" sign above a commercial business in downtown Johnson City. *Author's photo.*

1952 issue of *Look* magazine. It would take several more years for the stain of its seedy past to be removed from the image of Johnson City.

These days, much of the original downtown district remains largely intact, including many of the former speakeasies from the period. There has been a slow acceptance, if not a full embrace, of the Little Chicago nickname and of references to Al Capone. Businesses, restaurants paying homage and even a Little Chicago festival have sprung up in recent years.

The Bunch Gang

As already noted earlier, the Great Depression combined with Prohibition led to an explosion of illicit moonshining and bootlegging in the hills of East Tennessee. Poverty and alcohol have a long history as partners throughout American history, and this era was no exception. Towns and communities that had never before experienced such coordinated lawlessness saw an epidemic of activity that led many folks to choose to go down a dark path. One of the most storied tales to come out of the area is the account of the Bunch Gang from Claiborne County. Claiborne County lies smack in the middle between Harlan, Kentucky, and Knoxville, Tennessee, along the infamous "Thunder Road" bootlegging highway. Normally a sleepy farming and mining community, during the mid-1930s Claiborne gave birth to one of the most notorious outlaws about which stories and legends have been told throughout the years: a young country boy named Clarence "Pee Jem" Bunch.

Clarence Bunch was born on August 11, 1911, into a poor Appalachian family in an area of Caney Valley in Claiborne County aptly known as Bunchtown. His early years were relatively nondescript, as he lived a typical farming life filled with hard work and little reward aside from an occasional swig of whiskey. Bunch's family was already struggling to make ends meet when his father died at an early age, leaving his wife and children in a desperate position. The unfortunate passing of his father pushed young Clarence to find a way to help his family put food on the table. With few options available during this extremely trying time for the entire country, Bunch became involved in the one highly profitable local business that was hiring: the bootlegging industry. Bunch was a quick study and a fearless driver around the sharp, curvy mountain roads for such a young country boy with no real life experiences. He was brought into the local moonshine industry by more seasoned and established outlaws, including his mother's first cousin, C.T. Epperson.

Not long into his life of crime, Bunch was arrested for his involvement in a bank robbery in Ewing, Virginia, and thrown into the Cocke County Jail in Newport, where he would meet another young outlaw named Gus McCoig, a native of White Pine, who'd been jailed on a forgery charge. Bunch and McCoig struck up a friendship and soon hatched a plan to escape from their cell along with a third prisoner, John Campbell, which they accomplished on May 15, 1934. Legend has it that Bunch and McCoig formed a makeshift rope that they threw out a jail window down to Bunch's girlfriend, Nelle Payne, who was then able to sneak a gun up to the men by tying it to the end of the rope, which they then rolled back up. They used the gun to secure their freedom by surprising the attending jailer and shooting him in the arm before being let out. Once they were free, Campbell went his own way, while Bunch and McCoig stayed together as a team and would soon terrorize all of East Tennessee with their criminal exploits.

For her part, the striking blonde-haired, blue-eyed twenty-two-year-old Nelle Payne was arrested on the suspicion that she contributed to their escape by harboring, aiding and abetting her sweetheart, Clarence, and his gang. Police suspected that she traveled with the outlaws while dressed as a man and wearing dark goggles as a disguise. She denied the accusations and refused to give up any information on her boyfriend or the gang, saying, "I'd burn before I'd tell a thing."

Before long, Bunch and McCoig had recruited others into their group, which would soon become known all over the state as the "Bunch Gang." One of the main requirements to be a successful bootlegger in those days was a souped-up car able to outrun the law, and before long, the Bunch Gang had one in its possession to aid in its escape. Bunch and his cohorts graduated from bootlegging to robbery and soon began to terrorize the area from Claiborne County to Grainger County, Jefferson County and on down to Knoxville. Stories of the Bunch Gang robbing homes and businesses in an increasingly violent manner began to spread throughout the area. No crime was too small to be attributed to the gang members, as they were suspected in heists yielding as little as three dollars. They were said to not be shy about shooting their guns while also frequently pistol-whipping their victims. They were also said to employ a strategy of following unsuspecting motorists and then shooting out their tires at the opportune time. Once the intended victim pulled the car over, the gang would rob him or her at gunpoint before moving on to a new target.

Bunch is also thought to have led another jailbreak for members of his gang from a jail in Maryville using a similar trick employed in his own escape by tying guns to the end of strings dangled down from the prisoners. The guns were then used to free a total of fourteen inmates from the Maryville jail. Police throughout East Tennessee were increasingly frustrated and embarrassed by their inability to slow down the Bunch Gang's rampage. Handsome and engaging, Bunch took a liking to the limelight that came with his notoriety—this, in turn, made him a bigger target for law enforcement. Clarence Bunch was soon listed as East Tennessee's "Public Enemy No. 1," and a reward was offered for his arrest.

The long arm of the law began to put the squeeze on the Bunch Gang, and many of the members were either arrested or left to pursue a more honest trade. The tale of Clarence Bunch gets very sketchy at this point, as the details have been hotly debated ever since the fateful day of August 22, 1934. Many say that Bunch had been in talks for the week prior to this date with local law enforcement trying to negotiate terms for his surrender. Knowing his dire plight, in the days leading up to his demise Bunch is said to have been quoted as saying, "It is either the graveyard or the penitentiary for me, and I'll take the penitentiary." On August 22, Grainger County sheriff

Sam Roach informed the sheriff of Knox County, J. Wesley Brewer, that he had worked out a deal with Bunch for his surrender. They were to meet at a residence in Knoxville where Bunch was holed up with his mother's cousin and fellow bootlegger, C.T. Epperson.

Brewer, suspicious of Sheriff Roach, took over at the scene of the arrest and had his deputy, Tom Kirby, greet Bunch on the porch of the home with a .45-caliber Tommy gun. Chaos ensued at this point, as a scene unfolded that has been disputed ever since. Kirby and Brewer of the Knox County police claim that Bunch lunged for a pistol in the pocket of Sheriff Roach, which they claim he successfully grabbed and fired one shot into the air before being gunned down. Other local officers said that Bunch was unable to finish drawing the gun when he was mowed down in a hail of gunfire, first from the Tommy gun of Kirby and then from other officers' weapons. Still others claim that he didn't reach for a gun at all but rather was shot down in cold blood in an ambush. When the gunfire ended, somewhere in the range of twenty-three to twenty-seven shots had struck Clarence Bunch, sending him down in a heap on the porch.

In the aftermath of the shooting, Sheriff Brewer had Sheriff Roach of Grainger County arrested for aiding and abetting as the story of Bunch's death spread throughout the hills of East Tennessee. A picture of the corpse of Clarence Bunch was printed in the *Knoxville Journal* with a headline stating, "Bunch Meets Payoff: The Wages of Sin Is Death." His notoriety having spread during his crime spree, some have estimated that more than ten thousand people filed through to see his body—all the while folks discussed, speculated and disagreed over the why and how of his death. To this day, the real story of the death of Clarence Bunch is unknown and likely never will be.

One would think that such notorious characters would be seen as the embodiment of evil by local citizenry, but such is not the case for Clarence Bunch. In addition to the questionable circumstances surrounding his death, Bunch elicited sympathy due to the perception that he was, to a large degree, a victim of circumstances during a poverty-stricken time. Additionally, local stories such as one about Bunch robbing the Citizens Bank in New Tazewell have softened his image with many in the area. According to the story, a man named Monroe Poore was standing at a cashier's window when Bunch entered to rob the bank. According to the legend, Poore begged Bunch for mercy as the money was being used to pay off the large loan on his farm. Sympathetic to the man's pleadings, Bunch told the man to go ahead and pay the loan off and then get a receipt for his transaction as proof it was paid. Once the money was exchanged from Poore to the banker, Bunch proceeded to take it from the cashier.

In the years following the Bunch Gang's reign of terror, legends and rumors swirled that the various gang members had stashed much of the stolen money in different hiding places, from walls in homes to wads of cash buried along local riverbanks. A few treasure seekers throughout the years have even gone digging around based on a "hot tip" or a hunch looking for a payoff.

It may be true that "the wages of sin is death," but usually the legends of heroes and villains don't die when the person does; rather, they often take on a life of their own.

THE CATCHABLE BUT NOT FETCHABLE MOONSHINER

The stereotypical image of an Appalachian moonshiner usually conjures up thoughts of a wiry little old Caucasian man with a long, flowing beard wearing bibbed overalls. The story of Mahala "Big Haley" Mullins turns that image on its head in virtually every way. There haven't been many stories of prominent female moonshiners passed down through the years, but the legend of Big Haley is one well worth retelling. As any good fisherman will tell you, it is one thing to hook a large fish, but actually getting it in the boat is often the challenge. For Tennessee revenue officers, Mahala Mullins is the big fish that got away in this tale.

Mahala Mullins was a member of the Melungeon racial group whose members resided in the Newman's Ridge section of Sneedville in Hancock County, Tennessee, during the mid-1800s. As one might guess, Mahala was given the nickname "Big Haley" due to her large physical size, with various reports estimating her weight as being anywhere between four hundred and seven hundred pounds. It has been speculated that she suffered from either the disease elephantiasis or a thyroid condition that resulted in her massive weight gain. According to news reports from the period, Mahala gave birth to at least eighteen and possibly up to twenty children with her husband, John Mullins. Upon John's death, Mahala and the family had very few options for making additional money to provide for their needs beyond their subsistence farming.

One thing Mahala and her sons knew well was how to make some very desirable moonshine. They began to market their spirits to locals, but it didn't take long for word of their unique brews to spread, especially their popular apple brandy. Openly selling it by the jug or by the drink from a "community dipper," she kept a cask of whiskey beside her along with tin cups and measures. It didn't take long for the local authorities to hear of Big Haley's popular, but illegal, operation. A warrant was issued for her arrest, and this is where things began to get complicated. Mullins wasn't hard to find, as it has been said she never traveled farther than a three-mile radius during her entire time on this earth. By this stage in her life, Big Haley was confined to sitting in a chair due to her enormous weight. She spent day and night unable to rise under her own power, making her an even easier target to nab.

The revenuers made their way to her home, which was located in a sloped and rural part of the county, making it virtually impossible to reach by wagon. The officers informed Big Haley of the charges being brought against her for illegally making and selling moonshine. She cheerfully confessed her guilt and offered to let them take her in to face the charges. The real problem quickly surfaced, as the officers were at a loss as to how to get her out of the house and back into town to face the charges. Too wide to fit through the door, the men finally gave up and retreated back off

The Mahala Mullins Cabin in Hancock County, Tennessee. *Brian Stansberry, via Wikimedia Commons.*

the mountain, humbled in defeat. The same scenario played out over and over again, with somewhere in the vicinity of a dozen warrants issued for her arrest over the years, with no one figuring out a way to actually enforce them. They would have had to take out a portion of the walls to the house in order to get her out; however, they weren't legally authorized to damage the home. Even had they been able to remove her from the home, she lived at the top of a steep ridge, and the nearest railroad was sixteen miles away, creating other logistical issues. It was during this time that a deputy returned empty-handed and famously described Big Haley as being "catchable, but not fetchable."

To her credit, Big Haley never denied that she sold or that she would continue to sell her homebrew after they left her residence. Jovial, engaging and loquacious, Big Haley enjoyed company and would talk at length to anyone who came for a visit. Having been born and raised in a moonshining culture, she saw nothing morally or legally wrong with her side business and continued to sell until her death at the age of seventy-four on September 10, 1898. It has been said that when she died, the chimney in her house had to be removed to make enough room to take her body out for burial. Big Haley Mullins is considered to be the most famous Melungeon of all time and, as such, has been the subject of many stories and legends through the years in the Hancock County area. It seems appropriate that Big Haley Mullins, who was a large woman while she was living, is even larger than life in her death.

Part IV
Spooky Places of East Tennessee

Bethesda Cemetery and Church

Morristown, Tennessee, is home of the Bethesda Church and Cemetery, which has several tales of haunts and ghost stories attached to it. The church was built in 1835 and once served as a hospital for wounded Confederate soldiers during the Civil War. Several of the wounded soldiers passed away inside the church from their injuries and are buried at the cemetery.

The church and cemetery are said to be haunted by spirits thought to aggressively protect the area. There have been numerous reported Confederate ghost sightings both inside and outside the church. The church building is now boarded up, and some of the Rebel spirits are said to be trapped inside. The ghosts outside roaming the cemetery are said to be particularly hostile toward visitors from the North. If a Yankee accent is spoken in the cemetery, it is likely to provoke a reaction from one of the Rebel ghosts on duty. The Yankee visitor might experience a violent shove in the back or take an unexpected spill onto the ground at the hand of a mysterious unseen force. The Confederate ghosts generally stay in the area around the church, generously leaving the rest of the cemetery open to other haunts.

Another spooky tale from the cemetery includes hearing the voice of a weeping mother grieving the death of her newborn child. There have also been claims of the sound of a baby crying deep in the night near

The entrance to Bethesda Church and Cemetery near Morristown. *Author's photo.*

The Bethesda Church, which is said to be haunted by the ghosts of Confederate soldiers. *Author's photo.*

Grave of the unknown Confederate dead at Bethesda Cemetery. *Author's photo.*

Grave of an infant with a toy puppy dog. *Author's photo.*

Close-up of the inverted pentagram inscribed on the footstone of one of the graves. *Author's photo.*

the spot of the burial. The child is said to have died in infancy due to the spread of one of the many diseases that wreaked so much havoc in the days before advances in modern medicine. The baby died in the 1800s, yet its mother still wails in mourning for her lost child, proving that a mother's love never ends. The sound of crying is said to become more pronounced and hysterical if a small child is in the area, as it reminds the mother of her loss.

There also is said to be a local lady buried at the cemetery who is rumored to have practiced witchcraft and sorcery during her lifetime. Her footstone is marked with an inverted pentagram, and strange noises have been claimed to have come from her grave. The sounds of scratching and violent thrashing are said to come from deep in the earth. It has been speculated it is the sound of the witch trying to claw her way out of the ground. A closer inspection of the pentagram indicates it is possibly a symbol used by the Order of the Eastern Star (OES), a division of the Freemasons dedicated to women.

CHRISTOPHER TAYLOR HOUSE

A lot of houses are said to be haunted, but precious few can say they are occupied by the ghost of a former president of the United States. The Christopher Taylor House is the oldest standing house (built circa 1777) in Jonesborough, Tennessee, and is rumored to be haunted by the ghost of our seventh president, Andrew Jackson.

The home was moved from its original location about one mile out of town to its current spot in the downtown area. Fortunately, the ghost of President Jackson was able to relocate with the home, as he is still reportedly seen from time to time by folks in Jonesborough. Having earned the nickname "Old Hickory" for his toughness ("tough as hickory wood"), displayed during the Battle of New Orleans during the War of 1812, Jackson spent several months in the house boarding with the Taylor family early in his career as a lawyer just prior to serving in the military.

Local legend says that Jackson's ghost has been seen walking up to the house before suddenly passing straight through the door into the house. His spirit has also been seen leaving the residence and heading in the direction of the nearby courthouse before suddenly disappearing into thin air. He is described as a tall, lean figure wearing a black hat, trench coat and wading

The Christopher Taylor House in Jonesborough. *Author's photo.*

boots with accompanying white pants and is occasionally said to be riding atop a white horse.

Andrew Jackson apparently is more active these days than when he was alive, as his spirit has also been said to haunt his Nashville home, known as the Hermitage. Old Hickory hasn't allowed the inconvenience of a thing such as death slow him down in the afterlife.

NETHERLAND INN ROAD

If haunted places are your thing, the Netherland Inn Road connecting Kingsport to Church Hill is a short five-minute drive between three of the most well-known stories of ghostly activities in East Tennessee (Sensabaugh Tunnel, Rotherwood Mansion and Netherland Inn Road). The area near the road's namesake, Netherland Inn, is said to play host to the ghost of Hugh Hamblen, a local man who had his life cut short in a tragic auto accident. Unlike many other ghosts, Hugh Hamblen appears to help the living rather than trying to frighten or hinder them.

The story of Albert "Hugh" Hamblen dates back to a foggy and rainy downpour during the early morning hours of Sunday, November 17, 1922. The Netherland Inn Road lies along the Holston River and tends to attract a lot of fog coming in from the waterfront when it rains, so these conditions weren't unusual. The Saturday night of the sixteenth saw Hugh's son Charlie attend a dance in Church Hill that went on late into the night. As he was driving home with four other boys after the dance, Charlie was involved in an auto accident on the Rotherwood Bridge that sent him and the other passengers to the Riverview Hospital. Hugh was highly regarded as a father (with seven children), so it was no surprise that he rushed to the hospital to check on his injured son.

Hugh got to the hospital, where he nervously waited for word on the status of his young son. Two of the other young men were pronounced dead at the scene of the accident, leaving the other families to worry for the fate of their sons. Fortunately, Charlie's injuries were determined to not be life-threatening; though relieved, Hugh stayed by his son's side all night. Very early the next morning before daybreak, he discovered that the other two boys with Charlie had also perished, leaving his son as the only survivor. The terrible news left him mourning for the loss of the other boys while still being very grateful that his own son's life was spared.

View of the Netherland Inn Road, with the inn in the background. *Author's photo.*

At the insistence of other family members, Hugh decided to go back home to try to catch up on some sleep. The early morning hours saw the same dense fog and rainy conditions as the night before. Just as he was crossing the road to get to his car, Hugh looked up to see oncoming headlights headed straight in his direction. He threw his hands up to motion the oncoming car to slow down, but to no avail. The car barreled into Hugh without even slowing down, which sent him flying down an embankment gravely injured. He was taken to the hospital, where his injuries proved to be too much to recover from, and he passed away on November 20. It was later discovered that the driver of the car that struck Hugh had been a young and very inexperienced girl who was, understandably, distraught and quite shaken by the horrific tragedy. Charlie Hamblen physically recovered from the accident but, feeling a strong sense of guilt, carried the emotional weight of his father's death for the rest of his life.

On a foggy night just a few years after the tragic events, a driver reported seeing a man standing on the side of the road as he approached the area. The driver later stated that the middle-aged man, who was wearing a dark fedora and trench coat, had stepped out right in front of his oncoming car and began frantically waving his hands for the vehicle to stop. The driver slammed on his brakes to stop, but the car skidded out of control on the wet road and plowed into the man, sending him flying through the air. The panic-stricken driver rushed to get out of his car and then searched all over for the man he was sure he had just struck with his vehicle. He was never able to find any sign of the pedestrian, nor did a follow-up search conducted by the police. Additionally, no one fitting the man's description was ever reported missing.

The driver's story of seeing what appears to be the ghost of Hugh Hamblen was the first of what has been said to be well over one hundred separate accounts of seeing the apparition. The stories usually take place on stormy nights in a dense fog; the driver sees a man wearing the same trench coat and fedora, standing in the middle of the Netherland Inn Road and waving his hands for the driver to slow down the vehicle.

ROTHERWOOD MANSION

Kingsport, Tennessee, is one of the best (or worst, depending on your viewpoint) places around to find chilling ghost stories, and none is more haunting than the tale of the Rotherwood Mansion. The mansion was built high on a hill just above the banks of the north fork of the Holston River in 1818, before Kingsport was officially named Kingsport and was still known as Rossville. Rotherwood Mansion was built by Reverend Frederick Augustus Ross, who owned a sprawling plantation in the area and who was the namesake for the town at the time.

Frederick Ross's wife gave birth to a lovely daughter named Rowena, who by all accounts grew up to become a beautiful and very popular young lady. Rowena was the apple of Frederick's eye, and he saw to it that she enjoyed the finer things in life and had her educated in the most reputable of schools in New York and Philadelphia. Upon graduating, Rowena returned home to Rotherwood a refined and elegant socialite from her time away. For all her blessings early in life, Rowena's adult years would be cursed with tragedy and misfortune.

Shortly after returning home, the much-pursued Rowena was smitten with the love of her life, to whom she became engaged to be married. A lavish wedding was planned, and as her big day approached, Rowena couldn't have been any happier or more optimistic for her future. Tragically, her nuptials were not to be, as her fiancé drowned when his boat capsized while he was out fishing in front of Rotherwood Mansion, much to the shock and horror of his onlooking soon-to-be bride. The psychological blow brought on by witnessing this tragedy sent young Rowena into a reclusive downward spiral during which she seldom left home for the following two years.

After the two years passed by, Rowena finally was emotionally able to begin dating again and soon fell in love with a wealthy young man named Edward Temple from Knoxville. Soon, their relationship progressed to the point where they announced their engagement to be married. As evidence of the often cruel hand of fate, not long after their marriage and the birth of their daughter, Theodosia Ross Temple, Edward contracted yellow fever while in New Orleans and soon succumbed to the devastating disease, leaving young Rowena an inconsolable widow and single mother. The repercussions from this second loss sent Rowena down the dark path of depression once again.

Finally, after a few more years passed, Rowena got married to a new suitor, Wescom Hudgins. The wedded bliss wouldn't last, however, as Rowena had never truly recovered from her earlier traumas. When her daughter was a mere six years old, Rowena took her own life by drowning after walking into a river while living in Huntsville, Alabama. Some speculate that she was lured to her death while sleepwalking during a vivid dream of her first fiancé. Others say that she never overcame the depression brought on by her earlier losses that left her shattered. Rowena left behind her husband and daughter to try to come to grips with the loss of their wife and mother.

The ghost of Rowena relocated back to Kingsport, as she has been seen for almost two centuries along the grounds of the Rotherwood Mansion. Some have even seen her walking on the Holston River. She is always said to be wearing the white wedding dress in which she had planned to be married to her original fiancé. Her ghost has been locally referred to as the "Lady in White," and many think she is still roaming the area looking for her first fiancé, her one true love.

Misfortune would also befall Reverend Frederick Ross, as he ran into financial trouble due to an unwise investment in a cotton factory and was soon forced to sell the Rotherwood Mansion in 1853. The deed transfer would be the end of the Ross family's ownership of the property, but it was only the beginning of the nightmares that have long cursed the property. A fine man of faith, Reverend Ross had never taken pay for his preaching while in Kingsport. He sold the property without bitterness or regret, as his financial situation forced him to move to Chattanooga to make a living as a paid preacher. The purchaser of the estate was a slave owner with quite an opposite reputation, known for being quite surly and unreasonable. This man, Joshua Phipps, was also said to be quite barbaric and sadistic to his slaves, as he had a whipping post erected inside the property for their discipline.

Phipps was aided in his cruelty by his black mistress, who is said to have once been a slave herself. As Joshua Phipps was a slave driver in the truest sense of the term, his brutal reign of terror was successful in making the productivity of the plantation flourish in the years leading up to the Civil War. However, this would come to an end in 1861, when Joshua Phipps contracted a mysterious and fast-acting disease that made him bedridden with a high fever. While he continued to get sicker, he ordered a slave to stand by his bedside to help cool his fever with a fan. One night, as Phipps lay sleeping, the slave tending to him would later claim that a swarm of flies entered the room and proceeded to completely fill his mouth and nostrils. The flies were so thick that Phipps couldn't breathe, and they eventually suffocated him before leaving out the window. Upon Phipps's death, the remaining slaves killed his mistress in retribution for her part in their misery and then had her body buried in an unmarked grave somewhere on the estate.

It has been said that a large crowd gathered to attend Phipps's funeral ceremony at the estate, turning it into a great spectacle. As the hearse carrying Phipps's coffin was making its way up the hill, the horses pulling the weight began to have trouble. Dark clouds began to quickly move into the area around this same time as a thunderstorm neared. While the clouds grew darker, a large black dog suddenly popped out of Phipps's coffin and ran down the hill before disappearing out of sight as the crowd looked on in shock and horror. At this same time, the rain began to pour down in sheets, and the coffin was quickly buried; the funeral goers hastily left the area seeking shelter from the rain.

One ghost is usually the quota for a home, but Rotherwood Mansion is now said to be "blessed" with four: the ghost of the "Lady in White," which is tame by comparison; the ghosts of Joshua Phipps and his mistress, said to cause mayhem and havoc by removing covers from people who sleep there, laughing maniacally and, occasionally, giving guests an aggressive shove or two; and finally, the black "Hound of Hell" that can be heard howling on rainy evenings while prowling the estate.

Following the death of Joshua Phipps, Rotherwood has seen a series of different owners, including at one point being used by the United States Army prior to and during World War II. John B. Dennis, one of the most influential politicians in developing Kingsport as the "Model City," owned the property for a time as well. The Rotherwood Mansion is currently in private ownership and is not open to the public. Ghost sightings are still occasionally reported in the area around the Rotherwood estate, but apparently the new owner has made peace with them.

Sensabaugh Tunnel

One local haunt in Kingsport is the Sensabaugh Tunnel, which is just down the road from the Netherland Inn and the Rotherwood Mansion. Just off the Netherland Inn Road and onto Big Elm Road, the drive to the tunnel goes along a lonesome, narrow road just above the Holston River. The tunnel itself is covered with graffiti and marked with "No Trespassing" and "Keep Out" signs. It has long been said to be one of the most haunted places in Tennessee, with numerous tales of paranormal activity.

The tunnel dates back to the 1920s and has so many different legends attached that it is difficult to narrow them down. One frequently told story is about a family named, unsurprisingly, Sensabaugh. According to this story,

The "real" Sensabaugh Tunnel. *Author's photo.*

Left: Sensabaugh Hollow road sign leading to the "other" Sensabaugh Tunnel. *Author's photo.*

Below: The Click Tunnel, which has recently inherited many of the tales of the Sensabaugh Tunnel. *Author's photo.*

a drifter entered the Sensabaugh home for the purpose of robbing them only to be confronted by the Sensabaugh father. The would-be robber then grabbed the Sensabaughs' infant daughter from her crib and used her as a hostage to escape. Once free, he had no use for the baby, so he decided to rid himself of the unneeded baggage by drowning it and then leaving the lifeless body in the tunnel.

Another story goes that the Sensabaugh father went mad and butchered his entire family in a crazed rage one night. Once he came to his senses, he dragged their lifeless bodies inside the tunnel to hide them in an attempt to try to cover up his actions and avoid prosecution. Yet another story tells of an unsolved murder in which the body of a murdered pregnant teenage girl was discovered inside the tunnel. The girl's body had been stabbed multiple times, leaving her mutilated and unrecognizable to the police. The murder was never solved, nor was the girl's body ever conclusively identified, leaving it a great mystery.

The Sensabaugh Tunnel has had numerous claims of people hearing a baby's cries coming from inside the empty tunnel, the sound of a wailing young woman's voice, glimpses of Mr. Sensabaugh and a young woman around the tunnel near vehicles and a host of other tales. One of the most prevalent claims is that if you drive your car into the tunnel and turn off the ignition, it will not restart, as something will have killed the battery.

Which story is the truth? Likely none of them, as no news or police reports have ever been produced to corroborate any of the stories. In fact, these days many people can't agree on which tunnel is the real Sensabaugh Tunnel. The traditional Sensabaugh Tunnel is now almost impossible to reach by vehicle, as the road passes it by and the tunnel is often flooded. Just down the road in Sensabaugh Hollow is what is locally known as the "Click Tunnel," a tunnel that is very similar to Sensabaugh and has the same type of graffiti covering it. Conveniently, the Click Tunnel is still drivable, so many people have "moved" the story down the road for their paranormal experiences. Perhaps they are both haunted, as a fit ghost could easily make the trip between the two tunnels.

The Steel Bridge of Elizabethton

Elizabethton, Tennessee, is a small city in East Tennessee that serves as the county seat of Carter County. Elizabethton is a beautiful place to visit, as it is home to the Sycamore Shoals State Park along with a host of other historic attractions from the days in which it was inhabited by Native Americans and, later, by early pioneers of the United States. The rural landscape in the area makes for a great Sunday drive to soak up the beauty of the surrounding mountains. While out driving in Elizabethton, you may end up going through Siam Valley into the Stoney Creek community, which can be a very pleasant experience provided you don't end up with an unexpected passenger.

The Steel Bridge Road sign in the Siam Valley section of Elizabethton. *Author's photo.*

The Watauga River Bridge was known as the "Steel Bridge" to locals due to its steel construction. It didn't take long for the area below the scenic and peaceful steel bridge to became a popular hangout spot for young couples seeking some intimate alone time. In the early 1930s, Tom Jackson and Wanda Smithson were lovers who were among the many to use the spot for their makeout sessions.

One fateful night, Tom went to call on Wanda, whose family lived only three hundred yards from the bridge. They walked out to the spot underneath the bridge to be alone so they could talk and maybe sneak in a kiss or two, like young couples do when they're in love. They hung out under the bridge until about 10:00 p.m. before deciding they should get back home, as it was getting late.

Tom helped Wanda to her feet, and just as they turned to leave, they caught a glimpse of a dark, shadowy figure headed in their direction. At first they assumed it was just another couple coming to the area, as it wasn't uncommon for others to use it for the same purpose. The figure continued straight in their direction, and before they could react, it suddenly lunged at Wanda, stabbing her deep in the chest. She fell to the ground dead without even uttering a sound, completely blindsided by the attack. The assailant then turned his attention to Tom, who valiantly fought back despite being stabbed multiple times.

Tom was able to get away and made his way up the embankment and onto the Steel Bridge. A car happened to be crossing the bridge at this same time, and Tom desperately opened the rear door and threw himself into the backseat. The driver sped off as Tom clung to life while bleeding profusely from his wounds on the way to the hospital. Tom was able to relay the story of what had transpired to the police before he bled out and died that night.

The police went to the bridge to search for the attacker and to recover Wanda's body—neither was ever found. It was as if nothing had ever happened. They spent the next year searching for clues to what had happened that night, but to no avail. The case remains unsolved to this day. The story, however, doesn't end there.

The first report of anything odd happening in the area took place in 1977, when a sheriff's deputy from Gate City, Virginia, reported an unnerving encounter while crossing the Steel Bridge. He stated that he was driving alone across the bridge when suddenly his passenger door was flung open and then just as quickly slammed back shut. He hit the brakes and opened his door to get out, but when he opened the door, his interior light came on,

Remnants of the old Steel Bridge, which has been demolished. *Author's photo.*

revealing a frightening sight. He looked down and noticed that the passenger seat had a large indentation, as if someone were still sitting in it. He then noticed movement in his rearview mirror, and when he looked up, there appeared to be a dark, shadowy figure standing on the bridge behind him. He got out of the car, but the figure had disappeared by then, leaving him confused and frightened. He drove straight to the police station, where he gave a statement to the local authorities.

Since then, there have been numerous reports of similar activities in the area. No one knows what triggers these occurrences, but they all happen well after dark and the experiences described are usually quite similar. Perhaps Tom Jackson's spirit keeps returning to seek a measure of peace, or it is a posthumous attempt to escape his murderer. Maybe it was all a coincidence or people's minds playing tricks on them. In any case, the bridge has been torn down, leaving only remnants of where it used to be located. A new, modern bridge has been added just down the road. So far, no reports have been made of any unwanted passengers on the new bridge.

THE BLEEDING MAUSOLEUM OF CLEVELAND

The John and Adelia Thompson Craigmiles family were quite prominent in Cleveland, Tennessee, during the nineteenth century, having made their fortune in the mercantile business. John and Adelia were parents to a daughter named Nina, who stole the hearts of the family with her sweet disposition. Nina's maternal grandfather, Dr. Thompson, was among those smitten with little seven-year-old Nina, and they would often go on for long walks or short buggy rides together around town. One of these carriage rides ended in an unfortunate tragedy that led to a lingering reminder that has lasted to this day.

October 18, 1871, began like any other day in the lives of the Craigmiles family, with Dr. Thompson taking young Nina out for a ride around town. They hadn't been riding for long when Dr. Thompson mysteriously lost control of the buggy, which resulted in the carriage being pulled in front of a train. The train plowed into the side of the buggy, throwing Dr. Thompson to the ground unharmed. Young Nina, however, was not as fortunate, as she was killed instantly by the impact of the collision.

The family grieved at their great loss, and eventually her father decided to build a church to honor the life of his precious daughter. The family was

Episcopalian and, as such, began to construct the first official Episcopalian church in Cleveland, which would become known as the St. Luke's Episcopal Church. The name of St. Luke was chosen due to the day of Nina's death, October 18, coinciding with the day the Feast of St. Luke is celebrated. The church was completed on October 18, 1874, on the third anniversary of Nina's death. Soon after the church's completion, the Craigmiles family broke ground on a magnificent mausoleum wherein Nina's body would be given its final resting place. The finest Italian marble was imported for the project, as John Craigmiles would spare no expense in the construction. Four-foot-thick walls were accentuated with a marble spire leading up to a cross inside the memorial, which stands at just over thirty-seven feet tall. Once built, Nina's body was placed inside a marble tomb located in the center of the mausoleum.

Soon after Nina's body was placed inside the mausoleum, a strange and unexplainable phenomenon began to appear, as the marble began to develop crimson red streaks in it. Not long after Nina's death, the Craigmiles family would experience the loss of another child, this time an infant son who died during childbirth. He was also buried in the mausoleum alongside his sister. In 1899, John Craigmiles lost his life due to blood poisoning resulting from an infection that developed after taking a fall on an icy roadway. John Craigmiles was also buried inside the mausoleum next to his children. Tragedy would soon find the family again, as Adelia, who had since remarried, was struck by a car while crossing a street in Cleveland in September 1928. Adelia was interred with her children and her first husband inside the mausoleum at St. Luke's Episcopal Church.

The crimson streaks in the marble grew larger and darker with each tragic death and burial of a member of the Craigmiles family. Locals began to believe these crimson streaks to be the blood of the tragic Craigmiles family members seeping from the mausoleum in a supernatural display of mourning. These "bloody" streaks are said to have resisted all attempts to have them cleaned and removed. Some people say that the streaks were caused by small traces of lead, which can be found in marble. It is believed that this lead can turn red with extended exposure to the elements, which may explain the mysterious streaks. The streaks are visible to this day, bringing many visitors to the mausoleum for an in-person look. Whether from a supernatural mourning or just an explainable chemical reaction, the crimson streaks at the mausoleum at St. Luke's Episcopal Church have long kept the life and story of Nina Craigmiles alive—just as John Craigmiles intended when he built it.

THE DEVIL'S LOOKING GLASS

The Nolichucky River flows along for 115 miles through the peaceful hills and valleys of the Appalachian Mountains of East Tennessee on down into the French Broad River in Western North Carolina. Along its route, the Nolichucky passes through the heart of Unicoi County in East Tennessee, where the legend of the "Devil's Looking Glass" originates.

The Devil's Looking Glass is a wall of rocks looming ominously on the mountainside several hundred feet above the Nolichucky just outside Jonesborough and Erwin. The rock formation doesn't appear to be particularly ominous during the daylight hours, though. It is at nightfall when the face of the devil himself is said to be seen in the reflection of the moonlight against the rocks. If that sight alone weren't enough reason to be leery of the area, the number of stories of misfortune and hauntings in the vicinity has served as a warning through the years to steer clear.

The first stories alleging the presence of evil spirits dates back to the days when the Cherokee and Yuchi Indians roamed the area. Both tribes of Indians avoided the area, as they felt the presence of evil spirits dwelling around it. The Cherokees believed that a demon resided in a cave located halfway up the ridge to the Devil's Looking Glass. The demon was said to wreak havoc on any unfortunate soul who paddled his canoe to within striking distance or dared walk through the mountainside.

Another story dating back to the Cherokee era tells of a young Indian bride from the local tribe who received the dreaded news that her new husband had been killed in battle. The heartbroken young wife was so distraught that she climbed to the top of the Devil's Looking Glass and threw herself down over the jagged rocks below. Her ghost is still said to haunt the woods, where she can be heard wailing deep in the night, still mourning in agony for her lost love. Her spirit will not leave, as she waits to once again be reunited with her husband; until then, she will continue to grieve and cry out in anguish.

In the early part of the twentieth century, an elderly woman was rumored to practice witchcraft and Satan worship from her cabin near the site of the Devil's Looking Glass. Known simply as "ole Miss Wilson," she practiced her black magic at the behest of the evil spirits she summoned to her house for their dark powers. Chanting, cackling and unintelligible gibberish from multiple voices could be heard coming from the cabin at all hours of the night. It is highly unlikely that an elderly lady living in a shack deep in the hills of Unicoi County would be a high-energy "party girl," so the belief that she was a witchy woman seemed more plausible to most folks.

The Devil's Looking Glass stands as a shining example of how visual beauty sometimes masks a much darker backstory.

The Ghost of Fiddler's Rock

Music has a long, rich history in East Tennessee, with mountain music being a primary source of entertainment for the early settlers in the area. Banjos, guitars and mandolins have brought people together for fun at dances, community socials or just for sitting around the campfire. The fiddle is especially beloved for its unique, enchanting music that can enliven the spirits, as well as its sometimes mournful sound that can evoke deep emotions in the listener. The fiddle is considered to be one of the most difficult musical instruments to learn, as it requires hours and hours of disciplined practice to master. The legend of "The Ghost of Fiddler's Rock" concerns a young practitioner of the fiddle who met his demise in a most unusual way.

Stone Mountain near Mountain City in Johnson County. *Brian Stansberry, via Wikimedia Commons.*

Young Martin Stone earned a large following around the northeastern corner of Tennessee for his fiddling skills, honed in Johnson County during the late 1800s. A regular at social events ranging from weddings to funerals and everything in between, young Martin was a promising musician dedicated to his profession. He worked tirelessly to perfect his craft even on his off days, often hiking to the top of Stone Mountain, where he would sit and play for hours on end.

It was on one of these days at Stone Mountain that he began to develop a new, highly unusual fan club. As Martin began to play a slow, sorrowful song, he noticed a rattlesnake slowly slithering its way up close to him before it settled down to enjoy the music. Undisturbed by the presence of the rattlesnake, Martin continued to play his song when, before long, another snake appeared on the mountainside and slithered up close to the first one. Soon, more rattlesnakes joined the crowd to listen to the sweet sounds coming from the fiddle of Martin Stone, spellbound by the music as if he were an Egyptian snake charmer. The nighttime began to fall, finally prompting the snakes to begin to slowly leave in a retreat back to their homes for the night; Martin did likewise with his fiddle.

Martin Stone pondered the events of the day on his way home that night and came up with a plan for his next visit to Stone Mountain. The next week, Stone returned for another visit to see if he could once again draw out the rattlesnakes with his music. He quickly got his answer almost as soon as he put his bow to the fiddle and began to play. One by one, the rattlesnakes reappeared just as before, mesmerized by the rhythm of the fiddle playing. This time, however, Martin took advantage of the situation by drawing his shotgun up and firing at the rattlesnakes. The surviving snakes scattered in fear at the blast as Martin continued to fire away to kill as many as could be taken out. He then scooped up the dead snakes into the bag he had brought for the task. He took the snakes to sell their skin, which was in great demand for boots, belts and other fashionable clothing.

His first foray into the snakeskin business was a smashing success, so he decided to make it a cottage industry to subsidize his music career. Week after week, he returned to Stone Mountain, where he would repeat the same scenario of playing his fiddle followed by shooting the charmed snakes it drew out of the woods.

In a classic case of going to the well once too often, Martin's snake charming days came to an abrupt end near the end of that summer. He followed his same routine one warm Sunday afternoon by playing the fiddle and bringing out the snakes. This time, however, something

Rattlesnakes enjoyed the music of Martin Stone on top of Stone Mountain. *Carley J., U.S. Fish and Wildlife Service, via Wikimedia Commons.*

went terribly wrong as he played: the snakes didn't respond in the way they had before. Rather than being charmed, this time the sound of a chorus of rattles shaking drowned out the fiddle music. Martin Stone was unable to stop the anger of the snakes this time, as his playing seemed to only further enrage them. They began to strike at him, unleashing their deadly venom into his body, and soon the music stopped, replaced by the bloodcurdling screams of the dying young man. The entire mountainside soon became quiet and peaceful once again when the snakes were satisfied with their vengeance.

Family and friends began to worry about Martin Stone when he wasn't seen or heard from over the next few days. It eventually dawned on them to check the top of Stone Mountain, as it was common knowledge that he went there weekly to gather the snakeskin. The search party made the gruesome discovery of Martin's body riddled with snakebites. Curiously, his shotgun was found propped up undisturbed right beside his body, revealing that he'd made no attempt to stop the onslaught. No one is sure what caused the snakes to attack in such a coordinated manner, but one legend has it that the snakes turned the tables on Martin Stone; rather than being hypnotized by his music, they hypnotized him with their bewitching eyes. Believers of this theory say that it would explain why he made no attempt to reach for his gun.

Most folks in Johnson County stay far away from the area atop Stone Mountain these days despite the gorgeous view that can be seen from that vantage point. It is said that soft, lonely fiddle music can often be heard echoing from the mountains, but no one has ever been able to trace the source. In any case, if someone decides to follow Martin Stone's path of charming the snakes with their music on Stone Mountain, he should make sure his intentions are pure and his music is true, lest his life should end on a sour note.

Part V
Mysterious Creatures of East Tennessee

Ol' Green Eyes of Chickamauga Battlefield

A mysterious entity that has been spotted roaming around the Chickamauga Battlefield has spurred a few completely different legends, both of which are said to explain this phenomenon. The stories of "Ol' Green Eyes" attempt to give the backstory leading up to the appearance of the eerie glowing green eyes that have been seen throughout the battlefield. The sightings of Ol' Green Eyes have taken place for decades, and he is apparently not directly threatening but nonetheless frightening.

Since the Chickamauga Battlefield, located just outside Chattanooga, was the site of a major, bloody Civil War battle, it should come as no surprise that the first explanation involves the tragic death of a Confederate soldier. The soldier is said to have met his demise at the wrong end of a cannonball that blew his head clean off his body. The body was never found, but the head was recovered and buried in an unmarked grave at the battlefield. According to the legend, Ol' Green Eyes is the manifestation of the dead soldier's spirit walking around the battlefield desperately seeking to locate his body. In addition to the glowing green eyes, Ol' Green Eyes is said to moan as he moves through the park.

The other story offered to explain Ol' Green Eyes is far more sinister than a dead soldier; he is described as a creature that is half man and half monster. He walks upright and bears a physical resemblance to a human but also has the glowing green eyes, long hair like the fur of an animal and long fangs protruding from his deformed face. Multiple people have claimed to have seen this version of Ol' Green Eyes, said to predate the Civil War. Just catching a glimpse of Ol' Green Eyes has been blamed for accidents in which the driver of a car has had his or her attention diverted by the glowing eyes, leading to a crash.

WHAT LURKS AT THE BOTTOM OF THE TENNESSEE RIVER?

The Tennessee River stretches approximately 652 miles and passes through parts of three states (Alabama, Kentucky and Tennessee) as it majestically winds through the Appalachian Mountains. The historic river has been the subject of many stories and legends dating back to the days when Cherokee Indians roamed the area. One of the most often told legends is of a giant fish known as the Dakwa, a tale quite reminiscent of the story of Jonah in the Bible.

The story of the Dakwa begins with a group of Cherokee braves in a canoe paddling their way down the Tennessee River on a hunting expedition. Without warning, the calm waters of the Tennessee erupted as the giant Dakwa fish hurled itself through the air directly under the canoe, sending it flying. The Indians were ejected into the air, and the Dakwa swallowed one of them down and then disappeared with him down to the bottom of the river.

The other hunters went ashore, assuming that their fellow brave had met his demise in the belly of the Dakwa. Unbeknownst to them, the man was alive and well inside the fish but at a loss as to how to escape. He was frantically flailing around to find a way out when, miraculously, he was able to reach a sharp shell the fish had eaten. Using ingenuity prompted by desperation, he used the shell to cut into Dakwa in an effort to dig his way out. The fish began to become agitated and swam in an attempt to get relief from its "indigestion." The Dakwa eventually swam into shallow waters, and the Cherokee hunter was able to cut the rest of his way out.

Unharmed, the hunter then returned to his village, where he was surprised to discover the tribe was in mourning at the news of his "death." Once word of his survival spread, he soon became a hero in the tribe, who then held a large celebration in his honor. Permanent baldness was the only long-term consequence suffered from his time in the Dakwa, as the stomach acid had caused permanent damage to his scalp.

Another lingering story of the Tennessee River was possibly derived in some way from the story of the Dakwa. Shortly after the Cherokees had moved from the banks of the Tennessee River, another tale of a monster that dwelled at the bottom of the murky waters of the Tennessee began to spread. Rather than a fish, the subject of this legend was a massive sea serpent that was reportedly spotted in Chattanooga by a local fisherman, Buck Sutton, in 1822. He described seeing a monstrous serpent that rose up from the depths of the river before rapidly moving through the water and out of sight. An existing local legend noted that anyone who saw the sea serpent was doomed to meet certain death very shortly afterward. Sure enough, Sutton died just a few days after seeing the serpent.

In 1827, the serpent was seen again in the same vicinity by an unfortunate soul named Billy Burns who, sure enough, passed away very shortly after seeing the beast. A farmer named Jim Windom would become another victim, meeting his fateful end in 1829 despite his best efforts at praying and attending church regularly in an attempt to stave off the curse after his encounter. The descriptions from the men were all very similar; they spoke of seeing a blue- and yellow-colored serpent-like creature about twenty-five feet long with a massive head measuring over two feet and possessing a dark fin. The creature didn't appear violent or threatening when first seen; it was the aftereffects that did the men in.

Finally, sometime in the mid-1830s, the curse appeared to have been broken when a lady named Sallie Wilson saw the serpent, just as the men before her. She gave a similar description of the serpent, but unlike the others, she was able to live out a normal life after her encounter. Wilson's account would be the last sighting, as larger ships beginning to travel the Tennessee River and further development of the area are presumed to have driven the snake away from the area. In the decades following, there have been scattered, sketchy reports of seeing the sea serpent, but no one has been said to have passed away from their brush with the beast. No remains or evidence have ever been discovered to corroborate any of the sightings, but that hasn't deterred the belief in the Tennessee River's own version of the Loch Ness Monster.

THE WAMPUS CAT OF EAST TENNESSEE

One of the many legends taken from local Native American culture is the tale of the "Wampus Cat" of East Tennessee. Like most oral stories derived from the Indians, the story of the Wampus Cat is difficult, if not impossible, to trace back to its initial origin. The story has, however, remained remarkably consistent despite being passed down from one generation to the next for well over two centuries. The name "Wampus Cat" is derived from the word *cattywampus* (or *catawampus*), which means to be askew or not arranged in the correct order. As you will soon read, it is a fitting description of this fearsome creature that isn't quite human and isn't quite animal.

An old cliché says that curiosity killed the cat; however, in this tale, curiosity is what created the cat—or, more specifically, the Wampus Cat. The tale begins with a beautiful young Indian bride who begins to develop a growing curiosity about the activities of her husband and the other male members of their tribe. Her inquisitive mind kept preying on her and wouldn't let her rest until she finally decided to find out why their hunting trips were so secretive. She eventually hatched a plan where she would sneak out to spy on the men, a decision she would soon come to rue.

The young bride knew that her best bet was to mask herself to avoid being recognized as she prowled around the outskirts of their encampment. She wrapped herself up snugly in the pelt of a mountain lion in an attempt to avoid detection as she peered around a large rock to watch the men's nightly ceremony. The tribe of men began to carry out their sacred ritual of performing magic, chanting and dancing in worship of the Great Spirit that guided them.

As the young Indian woman slowly made her way closer to observe the proceedings, she tripped over an outstretched tree limb. The noise from her stumble drew the attention of some of the men in the camp, and she was quickly captured and brought before the tribe's medicine man to face punishment. The tribe's women were strictly forbidden from observing these rituals, so the consequences were harsh.

The medicine man decided that since she was trying to trick them by wearing the mountain lion pelt, the outcome would be to force her to spend the rest of her life trapped inside the skin of the beast. He transformed the young lady into a horrifying creature, half woman and half cat. She was then banished from the tribe and forced to live in the hills of East Tennessee, where she is said to roam to this very day. It has been said that on many nights she has been heard from deep in the hillside howling and crying out in mourning for her tragic fate. Many people believe that when her cries are heard, it is a spiritual sign that someone in the local community is going to die a tragic death within the next three days.

An unfortunate few people have claimed to have had personal encounters with the Wampus Cat through the years. She has been seen in the mountains from as far west as Chattanooga to along the Nolichucky River on the outskirts of Johnson City and Erwin in the eastern corner of Tennessee. The description of the beast tells of it having the sleek build of a mountain lion with short tan fur while walking upright on its two hind legs like a human. It is said to have pointy cat-like ears with paws rather than hands and feet, as well as a long tail. The Wampus Cat is said to have long, sharp fangs, which it flashes menacingly while hissing at anyone who comes in contact with it. Its eyes glow in the dark with a bright-yellow color, and it emits a terrible odor that is so ghastly it has been described as coming from the bowels of hell. Those who have been able to see directly into the Wampus Cat's face have described it as having the appearance of a beautiful young Indian woman. The people who have claimed to have seen it so far have all been males, which may just be a coincidence or, possibly, could also be the result of her harboring a grudge against men for their role in her unjust punishment.

The only things that have been known to ward off the Wampus Cat have been bright lights and quoting scriptures from the Bible. The aversion to Bible verses lends credence to the suggestion that the Wampus Cat is the product of a demonic curse. An often-told story involves a hunter who had an encounter with the Wampus Cat during which the man ended up being chased back into his cabin by the onrushing creature. The beast furiously attempted to break through the door, while the hunter tried to fend it off as best he could. Being a deeply religious man, the hunter's bunkmate began to pray and quoted scripture verses, which had the effect of driving the Wampus Cat back into the woods.

The story of the Wampus Cat is one of the oldest tales still being passed down from generation to generation in the area. It is often given blame when a campsite has been raided by a wild animal or when a family pet or farm animal suddenly goes missing. Whether a myth or reality, the Wampus Cat has served the purpose of spooking many men out of the woods safely back home to their wives.

U'TLUN'TA

The Cherokee Indians who once thrived in the mountains of East Tennessee have provided numerous legends that have been passed down through the years. One of the more haunting tales is that of U'tlun'ta, who is also commonly called "Spearfinger," a female evil-doer who roamed Chilhowee Mountain at the edge of the Great Smoky Mountains. The name "U'tlun'ta" roughly translates to "she had it sharp" in the Cherokee language, a very fitting description in reference to the long, spear-like forefinger on her right hand that she used to hunt her prey.

U'tlun'ta is said to have had skin made of stone, which served as protection from attack, as weapons would simply bounce off her hard shell, leaving her unharmed. She made quite a loud racket when she walked through the hills, as her stone skin made a sound like thunder that could be heard from a great distance. She was known to love singing and dancing, which made for a commotion that would sound like an earthquake or avalanche from afar. She also possessed great strength, as she was capable of picking up, moving, breaking and even fusing large rocks and boulders as part of her special abilities. U'tlun'ta was also able to shape her body into any form, although she usually chose to take on the form of a non-threatening elderly woman. Once she had chosen a form, she could not change into any other form until she was out of eyesight. She had an insatiable appetite for eating human livers (preferably those of young children) and used her ability to change forms to lure in her unsuspecting victims.

One of her favorite tactics was to change her appearance to resemble family members of children so that she could gain their trust and confidence before leading them to their demise. Once the child was thoroughly convinced, she would stroke the child's hair until he or she would drift off into a deep, peaceful sleep. U'tlun'ta would then take her spearfinger and surgically cut out their liver to feed her appetite. She would quickly and surgically stab her victims through the neck or heart to get to the liver while managing to not leave a scar or any other visible sign of the attack. In most cases, the victim wouldn't die immediately but would become sick several days after the attack before perishing mysteriously. One of her favorite methods was to infiltrate a home by killing a victim, hiding their body and taking on their appearance. She would then be able to take multiple livers as everyone slept, leaving an entire family wiped out at her hand—or, more accurately, her finger.

Once they figured out what was happening, the Cherokees became filled with paranoia and terror of the stealthy predator that was decimating their

The former site of Chilhowee village, now submerged by Chilhowee Lake. *Brian Stansberry, via Wikimedia Commons.*

tribes. The medicine man of the tribe put out guidelines to minimize her ability to penetrate their village. No one was to go into the woods or to fetch water alone, and strangers were looked at with great suspicion. Children were seen as the most vulnerable, so they were expressly forbidden from leaving the village for any reason and were taught to not implicitly trust female elders. Despite these cautionary measures, U'tlun'ta was able to claim additional victims, resulting in the need for more drastic measures.

A great council of tribes was called where the medicine man explained his theory for what was happening to other tribal leaders. They then discussed the need for a cohesive plan to defend their people from the menace. At the council, several hunters told of their encounters with an elderly woman with an oddly sharp finger whom they'd met while out in the woods. They now had a suspect but needed a plan for killing her to end the reign of terror. After much debate and discussion, the medicine man announced the strategy for capturing her. They surmised that she was attracted to fire, as it was a sign of an encampment where she would find humans and, with that, the livers she craved. The Indians decided to dig a huge pit over which they built a massive fire to draw her in.

As hoped, the smoke from the fire was irresistible to U'tlun'ta, and she was soon lured into the area. She was in her usual disguise of an elderly woman, and she had covered her right hand with a blanket to disguise her weapon of choice. She feebly approached the men and asked for help in a weak voice. Despite all the planning, some of the younger braves were confused and began to fall for the "helpless grandmother" routine. The medicine man was unfazed by her antics and promptly hurled a spear at her. The spear bounced off her stone skin and broke apart as it hit the ground. The other braves then snapped out of U'tlun'ta's spell and unleashed an attack on her upon witnessing what happened to the spear. One by one, she repelled the spears and arrows. The enraged U'tlun'ta then charged at the men with her spear-like finger extended to slash them. The trap worked, and she fell in the pit as she approached them; however, she was unhurt by the fall and proceeded to wildly swing her finger as she lashed out at the crowd gathered above the pit.

Suddenly, a titmouse bird flew down through the smoke and seemed to indicate to the braves to aim for U'tlun'ta's heart by singing a tune that resembled the Indian word for heart. They fired at U'tlun'ta's heart to no avail, as the weapons all bounced off her just as before. U'tlun'ta began to taunt the attacking Indians by cackling and threatening their lives despite her precarious position. The Indians were said to have taken their frustrations out on the titmouse bird by capturing it and cutting off its tongue to warn others that it was a liar. The titmouse flew away, never to be seen again. Directly afterward, a chickadee bird flew down from the sky and attacked U'tlun'ta's right hand. In a panic, U'tlun'ta balled her hand up into a tight fist to protect it while frantically flailing to fend off the bird. The men realized that there must be some reason why she was so protective of the palm of her hand. They then began to aim their attack directly at her right hand, which upset her greatly. Eventually, the hand was pierced, and U'tlun'ta slowly wilted and sank into the ground before she finally fell over dead to the cheer of the onlooking braves. The spearfinger that had wreaked so much havoc "twitched and was still," and it was later discovered that her heart was located in the same hand, tucked inside her palm. The horror of U'tlun'ta had finally ended, and the Cherokees were able to resume their normal lives.

In the aftermath of the attack, chickadee birds were thereafter seen as "truth tellers" and revered by the Cherokee Indians. A chickadee perched outside a home is believed to be a sign that a man who is away from home will return safely. The Cherokees named the site in Blount County where U'tlun'ta is said to have met her death "U'Tluntun'yi," which aptly translates to "the Spearfinger Place."

SKINNED TOM

Have you seen the ghost of Skinned Tom?
Long white bones with the skin all gone
Poor, poor, poor, ol' Tom
Wouldn't it be chilly with no skin on?

This nursery rhyme is probably not one anyone would want taught to their children in elementary school these days. The lyrics are also often seen as "have you seen the ghost of Tom?" in other parts of the country but have been altered to fit a local urban legend. Several urban legends have roots deep in the hills of East Tennessee, which leads one to question why they aren't called "rural legends." One such tale native to East Tennessee is the story of Skinned Tom, a playboy who chose the wrong woman to woo and paid the price for his sins in a most disturbing manner.

Tom was quite the ladies' man in the 1920s, with a reputation for seducing most any woman he pursued using his wit, charm and dashing good looks. Like most men with his ability to bewitch the opposite sex, Tom was never satisfied with one lady for long before he would move on to a new conquest. He would follow this same pattern of giving a new romantic interest his time and undivided attention to make her feel as though she was the only woman in the world to him. Once he got his jollies and sufficiently fed his ego, it was on to the next one.

He eventually ran out of women in his hometown, so he then began to venture over to the next town to look for a fresh crop of girls to excite him. He soon ran into a lady who would be the last notch on his bedpost, a gal named Eleanor. Eleanor was quite a striking figure, with blue eyes that sparkled, long blond hair that flowed down her shoulders and a body that would test the willpower of any man. They were a match made in heaven on paper except for one major drawback: Eleanor was already married to another man. Undeterred, Tom made a move on Eleanor, and like so many before her, it didn't take long before the two quietly became lovers.

Tom and Eleanor began to regularly meet after dark in a place known locally as "Lover's Lane" for its privacy and remoteness, making it a perfect spot for amorous couples to rendezvous. They met often and soon became more brazen with their encounters, which led to them becoming lazy about covering their tracks. As often is the case with such affairs, it didn't take long for the rumors to fly about Eleanor sneaking off behind her husband's back. The talk around town eventually made it back to her husband, leaving him in a fit of jealousy. Rather than confront his wife directly, he decided to do his own investigation to see if the stories were true.

The more he thought about his wife in the arms of another man, the more his blood boiled with rage. He came up with the idea to tell Eleanor that he was going out of town for the weekend on a business trip. Instead, he hid where he could watch the house to find out what his wife was up to while he was supposedly gone. Sure enough, it didn't take long before Tom pulled into their driveway to pick up Eleanor for yet another night out. They drove off, and this time the husband followed them at a safe distance. They soon pulled into Lover's Lane, where they proceeded to engage in their usual extracurricular activities.

Lost in the throes of passion, they were unaware that Eleanor's husband had approached Tom's car door. The husband violently jerked the door open, which greatly startled Tom and Eleanor. Upon seeing the husband clutching a hunting knife in his right hand, Tom began to beg for his life. He claimed to have no idea that Eleanor was a married woman, but his pleas fell on deaf ears as the husband yanked him out of the car. Fearing for her life, Eleanor ran away into the woods to escape her husband's vengeance. Tom wasn't as fortunate, as the husband began to surgically use the knife to literally "skin him alive." Tom's horrific screams rang out in the night air and echoed through the mountainside. He called out, begging for mercy from the brutal attack, but the husband wasn't about to grant him any relief.

Eventually, the husband had completely removed all of Tom's skin from his body and left him for dead. Satisfied with the result, the husband dropped his knife and then calmly got back into his car and drove himself to the local police station, where he confessed his crime of passion. The police raced out to the scene, assuming they would find the dead body of Tom; however, all they found when they got there was a mess of blood and skin but no victim's body or murder weapon. Despite combing the area for days, no further trace of Tom or the knife was ever found by the police.

It is local legend that the bloody skeleton of Skinned Tom still roams the area around Lover's Lane. Having learned a terrible lesson himself, Skinned Tom now seeks out cheating couples to serve as a warning to quit their philandering ways. He is rumored to still be carrying the knife that was used on him; he uses it to show would-be cheaters the consequences of life as an adulterer.

Part VI

Unexplained Phenomena and Other Legends and Lore

Melungeons

The history of the racial group known as Melungeons is a topic of much discussion, disagreement and mystery. Melungeons often display many physical characteristics usually associated with European heritage, such as angular facial features, combined with dark eyes, dark hair and dark skin normally associated with African American and Native American ethnicities. The prevalent belief is that they are what has been described as "tri-racial," combining European, African American and Native American ancestries. However, there has long been discussion that they are of Portuguese and possibly even Turkish descent as well. The Melungeons were originally found primarily in the Cumberland Gap area of Southwest Virginia, East Tennessee and eastern Kentucky, with notable populations in Hawkins and Hancock Counties in East Tennessee and Lee and Scott Counties in Virginia. A section of Hancock County known as Newman's Ridge is considered to be the heart of Melungeon heritage in recent times.

Melungeons have historically been considered "free people of color" who owned land and had voting rights. They were generally accepted in their communities and mostly assimilated save for the fact that they often were restricted in marriage due to laws penalizing the mixing of races. In more recent years, most Melungeons have become virtually indistinguishable from Caucasians due to the tendency to intermarry as social changes have made interracial marriage increasingly more accepted.

Above: Photo of Newmans Ridge Road in Sneedville, Tennessee. *Author's photo.*

Left: Abraham Lincoln. *Library of Congress, LC-DIG-pga-03167.*

Even the initial origination of the term *Melungeon* is a mystery, as some feel it is derived from the French word *mélange*, which translates to "mixture." Others think it is coined from the antiquated and obsolete English word *malengin*, which meant "bad intention/fraud/deceit." Yet another possibility is that it comes from the African word *melungo*, which was used as a derogatory word describing people of Portuguese and white backgrounds. The first known written use of the term came in 1813 in Scott County, Virginia, where a church recorded it spelled as "Melungins."

The term was itself once seen as a racial slur and was received with a negative connotation; however, that has since softened, as many now proudly self-identify as Melungeon. Playwright Kermit Hunter wrote the highly regarded *Walk Toward the Sunset*, in which Melungeons were portrayed in a romanticized light, which helped to develop a sense of pride in the heritage. Much speculation has been made regarding the likelihood of Melungeon ancestry in President Abraham Lincoln and possibly (though not as likely) Elvis Presley. Lincoln displayed many of the features associated with Melungeon heritage, including dark skin, dark eyes and sharp facial features. Melungeons are proof that the "great American melting pot" extends to the Appalachians.

SWIFT'S SILVER MINE

The story of Swift's Lost Silver Mine is one of the great legends and mysteries from early American history. The story dates all the way back to 1760, when an Englishman named Jonathan (also known as John) Swift is said to have discovered a large silver mine inside a cave in the Appalachian Mountains. The location of the mine has been the subject of much debate, research and speculation for more than 250 years, with no conclusive answer. The mountains of East Tennessee, eastern Kentucky and Southwest Virginia have been the most frequently rumored locations of the mine and the buried treasure.

The legend is based on a journal written by Jonathan Swift that claims he was led to a cave filled with silver ore by a man named George Munday. Munday had allegedly been held captive by the Shawnee Indians, from whom he had first learned of the vast silver deposit.

Another variation of the story claims that Swift discovered the cave while pursuing a wounded bear. Swift's journal goes on to claim that he returned to the cave for nine years mining the silver and then later burying some of it in other locations throughout the area. In 1769, Swift finally ceased mining it and then barricaded the cave due to the threat of Indian attacks as well as internal conflict between Swift and his crew. Before he could return to the mine, Jonathan Swift went blind and spent his final years in Bean Station, Tennessee. Upon his death, Swift is said to have left his journal along with a map describing the location of the mine to his caretaker in Bean Station, a widow known as Mrs. Renfro.

Jonathan Swift's journal gives descriptions that are somewhat generic and could apply to most any town. For example, some of the treasure is said to have been buried "by the fork of a white oak" and "in the rock of a rock house." Another reason for the uncertainty of the location is that there have been numerous variations of Swift's journal produced over time, creating further confusion. Jonathan Swift himself is the subject of much debate and speculation. Swift has been cast in different roles as a pirate, explorer, Indian trader and counterfeiter. Some stories claim that Swift murdered his crew at the end of their last excursion in the heat of greed and was cursed with the blindness that prevented him from ever re-locating the mine.

There has been some speculation about whether or not this Jonathan Swift even existed at all, as there is little historical data to prove his existence. One of the first people to discuss Swift's Silver Mine was Kentucky author John Filson, who was known for his writings about Daniel Boone. Some historians feel that Filson actually wrote the journal of Jonathan Swift as a work of fiction, having been inspired by the novel *Gulliver's Travels* by the Irish author coincidentally (?) named Jonathan Swift.

The East Tennessee versions of Swift's Silver Mine tend to focus on two primary areas: what is now the Big South Fork National River & Recreation Area in Oneida and the mountains surrounding the city of Jellico near the Cumberland Gap. Many people have searched in vain for the lost silver mines, including the famous Kentucky pioneer James Harrod, who in 1792 went on a search for the mine and never returned. Harrod's body was never found, and his family speculated that he'd been lured by the prospect of finding the silver into the woods to be murdered.

Like any good mystery, the story of Swift's Lost Silver Mine leaves more questions than answers: Where is the mine located? Was there ever really a mine? If so, why hasn't any substantial silver ore been found in the area? Did Jonathan Swift really exist? The search could go on for another 250 years.

THE GRASSY BALDS OF ROAN MOUNTAIN

Roan Mountain is part of the Roan-Unaka Range of the Appalachian Mountains and rises to an elevation of 6,285 feet at its highest point. Featuring five mountain peaks, Roan Mountain extends from Carter County in Tennessee on down into Mitchell County in North Carolina. Wildly popular these days for hiking, camping and other outdoor activities, Roan Mountain was long ago popular with Native Americans for the hunting opportunities provided by the varied wildlife roaming the land.

Roan Mountain is also home to one of the most baffling scientific mysteries of modern times: the phenomenon known as the grassy bald. A grassy bald occurs when a mountain summit lacks the trees and heavy forestry normally associated with a mountain in favor of grass, small shrubs or some other thick vegetation. The grassy balds on Roan Mountain allow for some of the most majestic panoramic year-round mountaintop views a nature lover could hope to witness. The cause of the balds has been a great mystery and subject of debate for decades, as there would seem to be no obvious scientific reason for their existence.

Theories and legends abound as to what has created these balds. Scientists have suggested that perhaps they were created in the prehistoric era when woolly mammoths, mastodons and other large creatures would have grazed on larger forestry as their food supply, clearing off these areas. This theory then goes on to expound that smaller animals such as bison and elk would have continued grazing on the vegetation to keep it free from trees after the extinction of the larger animals. Another common scientific theory is that the high elevation of the balds made them unsuitable for growth of trees and the like due to colder temperatures. The problem with this hypothesis is that it doesn't explain why two adjacent mountain peaks, such as Round Bald (with an elevation of 5,826 feet) and Roan High Knob (with an elevation of 6,285 feet), could have two vastly different topographies. Despite their proximity, Round Bald is a grassy bald with virtually no trees, while Roan High Knob is densely covered by a tundra-like spruce-fir forest. Yet another explanation offered up is that, over time, a series of lightning strikes ignited small forest fires in the drier areas of the mountains that burned off all the trees in the vicinity. There is no other evidence of fire damage in the area, which has called this theory into question.

In lieu of a concrete scientific explanation, several other theories and tales have sprung up to explain this unusual occurrence. One such legend attributes the balds to the work of the devil, who is said to have roamed through the mountains stunting the growth of trees with his cursed footsteps. Another legend comes from the Catawba Indian tribe and describes a major battle with the Cherokees in these areas. The blood lost by the Indians during this battle is said to have stained the rhododendrons a crimson color and cursed the ground on which the blood was shed. Many Native American artifacts have been discovered throughout the area, but no proof of any great battle has been found to date.

For now, the grassy balds of Roan Mountain remain an unsolved natural mystery. The full truth may never be discovered; in the meantime, that hasn't stopped a veritable forest of different theories and opinions from growing.

SNAKE HANDLING CHURCHES

And these signs shall follow them that believe; In my name shall they cast out devils; they shall speak with new tongues; They shall take up serpents; and if they drink any deadly thing, it shall not hurt them; they shall lay hands on the sick, and they shall recover.

—*Mark 16:17–18*

These biblical verses are the cornerstone of the religious practice commonly known as "snake handling" that has long been a source of fascination and mystery like few topics in Appalachian history. As it specifically pertains to the practice of snake handling, never before has a ritual that is practiced by so few come to be associated with so many. The persistent belief that snake handling is a common practice in East Tennessee or Appalachia is a myth and misconception.

The specific origin of snake handling is cloudy, as there have been individual instances of people using snakes in religious demonstrations off and on throughout history. They justify the use of snakes by taking a literal interpretation of the scriptures found in the Gospel of Mark 16:17–18 for inspiration. The true meaning of these verses has long been debated, as many say that they refer to the actions of the Apostles immediately following the resurrection of Jesus and are not meant to apply to all believers. Other biblical scholars believe that verses 9–20 of the Gospel of Mark weren't part of the original manuscripts of the Bible and hence aren't applicable.

The spread in popularity of snake handling into Appalachia is most often credited to a charismatic evangelist named George Went Hensley. Hensley underwent a religious experience in his late twenties during which he began to ponder his personal level of righteousness. He locked in on the verses in Mark 16 based on an experience early in his life that left a strong impression on him—he witnessed a lady handle a snake in a church service at a coal camp in Southwest Virginia.

Hensley further claimed that he asked for a sign from God while walking up a mountain when he came upon a rattlesnake and fell on his knees before it in prayer. He then scooped up the rattlesnake and placed it in a gunnysack to take back to show his congregation. He brought the snake to his next service, where he took it out of the sack, handled it himself unharmed and then challenged the congregation to do likewise as a show of faith.

Hensley then began to introduce this snake-handling practice as a regular part of his sermons as an ordained minister in the Church of God denomination. Hensley conducted revivals throughout Tennessee and, later, the Carolinas, Florida, Indiana, Kentucky, Ohio and Virginia, drawing crowds primarily made up of the families of farmers and coal miners. Soon Hensley's meetings began to draw large crowds for the spectacle as much as the message. He inspired other "disciples" of his ministerial style such as Raymond Hayes, who is often credited with the spread of snake handling into West Virginia.

George Hensley's popularity and influence was at its peak in 1922, when he opted to resign from his Church of God ministerial position due to "trouble in the home." Hensley went on to be arrested in 1923 for moonshining activity but would later escape by fleeing from the chain gang detail to which he'd been assigned. He hid out near his sister's farm in Ooltewah, Tennessee, before moving to Ohio, where he soon resumed his ministry. He then moved to Pineville, Kentucky, and built a new church, where he once again built a following based largely on his snake-handling practice. Hensley was never able to fully recapture his earlier popularity due to greater awareness of his checkered past of the moonshine arrest and the fact he'd been married four times (divorce is frowned on by the church).

Hensley spent the remainder of his life preaching and spreading his concept of the Bible. He was conducting an extended revival inside an abandoned blacksmith shop in Altha, Florida, when he gave what would prove to be his last sermon. Hensley was preaching and moving about the crowd with a venomous snake wrapped around his neck, as had become his custom. He went to put the snake back into its container when suddenly it bit him on the wrist. Hensley quickly became ill—experiencing excruciating pain and vomiting up blood. Despite pleas to get treatment from the congregation,

Hensley defiantly refused and instead implored the crowd to pray while telling them that their lack of faith was what had caused his suffering. Hensley would not recover and was pronounced dead the following morning on July 25, 1955, with the official cause of death being ruled suicide.

The practice of snake handling would live on past the death of George Hensley to this day. It has been speculated that there are still as many as 125 churches and up to five thousand practitioners of snake handling. Others have guesstimated that there are as few as 40 churches and five hundred practitioners. The actual number is impossible to verify, as most of the churches operate illegally in violation of state statutes outlawing the use of snakes in such ceremonies (snake handling is legal only in West Virginia). Additionally, most of these sermons are conducted in residential homes or makeshift abandoned buildings, making them even more difficult to track.

Another less discussed practice specific to most snake-handling churches is the belief that members can drink poison with no ill effects and touch fire without getting burned. The "poison of choice" is often strychnine, although they will also use battery acid or carbolic acid as well, which they drink down like some would take a shot of liquor. They will also use a candle or fill the top of a bottle with a rag, which they light and hold against their skin while praying, singing and dancing without getting burned. The churches maintain that members aren't forced to participate in any of the practices. Church members are taught to abstain from them unless they are "in the Spirit"—defined as being inspired by the Spirit of God to do these actions that would be deadly without his help.

Snake-handling churches are loosely affiliated with the Pentecostal faith, as they incorporate some of the same practices, such as speaking in tongues and laying hands on the sick. Most Pentecostals distance themselves from the snake-handling sect, as they reject the handling of snakes, drinking of poison and use of fire as accepted practices. Some people from outside the Appalachian region mistakenly lump the two faiths together, which can create the misconception of a larger contingent of snake-handling practitioners.

Tennessee passed a law in 1947 that made it illegal to own poisonous snakes following the death of five worshipers on different occasions over a two-year span. Snake-handling churches in East Tennessee have been on a long, steady decline, and there is a great possibility that they will become extinct as they become another victim of progress. These days, snake handling is commonly seen as something that adds character and mystery to our culture to make it more intriguing.

Unusual Town Names

There are many unusual town, community and road names throughout East Tennessee. Like most other folklore, the stories behind the names have been passed down orally for generations with little or no documented proof to back up these claims. Some of the stories are simple and logical, while others are a bit of a stretch to believe. Here are a few examples of the names and stories attached to them.

Nameless, Jackson County: There are various versions of how this community got its "Nameless" name. One story says that there was a big community gathering to discuss the name for the new post office that was going to be located in the area. The townsfolk couldn't agree on a name, and finally, after much debate, one piped up, "This here's a nameless place if ever I saw one, so leave it be." According to the story, the comment struck a nerve with others, who were tired of the whole debate and decided to make it stick. Another story claims that when residents sent in their application for a post

The road sign for Nameless, Tennessee. *Brian Stansberry, via Wikimedia Commons.*

office, they accidentally left the name for the post office blank. Supposedly, the United States Post Office Department sent back the application with "nameless" stamped on it, and the name stuck. Yet another story claims that it was going to be named "Morgan" after a local politician. The Post Office Department then claimed to have rejected it due to the possible name association with Confederate general John Hunt Morgan, as the post office was created in 1866, shortly after the ending of the Civil War. The official submitting the application is said to have written a letter back at that point saying if the chosen name wasn't going to be used, then the post office should remain nameless.

FIERY GIZZARD CREEK, GRUNDY COUNTY: One version of the story says that famous pioneer Davy Crockett burned his tongue while eating a turkey gizzard along the creek and then spit it out. Another version says it was named Fiery Gizzard when an Indian chief tossed a turkey gizzard into a fire while in peace talks in an attempt to capture the attention of the white men in attendance.

SODDY-DAISY, HAMILTON COUNTY: Here is another cloudy name history—the "Soddy" portion is said to possibly be an attempt at spelling the Cherokee word *Tsati*. The word was what the Cherokees used for the Muskogean Koasati Native Americans who lived in the area prior to the arrival of the Cherokees in the eighteenth century. Another version theorizes that the "Soddy" came from a local merchant named William Sodder, who ran a trading post in the area. The third version says that it is a reference to Soddy Creek, which was so named as a derivative of another Cherokee word, *Sauta*, which references the Echota Cherokee tribe. The "Daisy" part is thought to be in honor of Daisy Parks, daughter of the founder of the Daisy Coal Company, Thomas Parks.

TRADE, JOHNSON COUNTY: Trade was originally known as the Trade Gap in the eighteenth century for a trading post that served pioneers and Native Americans, where they could come trade furs and other merchandise.

HOHENWALD, LEWIS COUNTY: *Hohenwald* is a German word that simply translates to "high forest." Hohenwald was likely named by Swiss immigrants who settled in the Lewis County area in the late 1800s. There was also once a town named New Switzerland, but it has since been merged into Hohenwald.

ETOWAH, MCMINN COUNTY: Etowah is thought to have been named after a sign that was brought into town by a train crew from the Etowah River. On a side note, *etowah* is a Muskogee word that simply means "town."

FLAG POND, UNICOI COUNTY: The local folklore says that a young lady named Stefanne saw the flag flower Iris while walking along the edge of a pond. She described the area as the flag pond, and the name stuck for the entire area.

BONE CAVE, VAN BUREN COUNTY: Bone Cave is named from Big Bone Cave, which in turn was named for the discovery of bones inside the cave. A giant ground sloth was among the finds there. It is also rumored that children would go into the cave while tied to a rope and would occasionally bring out human bones from their explorations. The human bones were thought to be from a band of robbers that once used the area as its headquarters. The robbers would kill riders to steal their wares and horses, disposing of the dead inside the cave.

CALFKILLER, WHITE COUNTY: The Calfkiller River was named for a Cherokee chief who lived in the area when the first white settlers came about 1800. The Indian chief led frequent raids on the young cattle of these settlers. Another story says that Calfkiller was named due to the very cold stream of water that would often freeze young cattle that waded out in the waters. The calves would become numb from the cold, making them unable to leave the waters, and they would eventually drown. A third story involves a man who had a large herd of cattle that he led into the river only to see them get spooked; the entire herd drowned in a panicked stampede.

YANKEETOWN, WHITE COUNTY: A lot of folks mistakenly believe this place earned the name during the Civil War due to a large number of Yankee soldiers camping out in the area. It was actually named Yankeetown prior to the war for the high number of northerners who had moved into the area. Most all of the northerners fled the area when the Civil War broke out. Many attempts were made by southerners (who detested it) thereafter to change the name of the town, but none was ever successful, so the name lives on.

BOOGERTOWN, SEVIER COUNTY: Several competing stories have been offered to explain the origin of this name; however, they all revolve around a ghost (also known as a "haint" or "booger"). One story goes that it was so named for the mysterious killings of local livestock—said to be the work of a "booger." The other versions have some variation of local people being spooked by either a white, ghostly form seen at night or eerie sounds coming from the woods.

MOUNTAIN SUPERSTITIONS

Death Crowns

One of the more fascinating, and somewhat eerie, pieces of folklore in Appalachia is that of the feather "death crown." The death crown phenomenon occurs when a clump of the feathers inside a pillow takes the form of a crown after someone passes away. Feather pillows were quite the norm in yesteryear, so it wasn't uncommon for the deceased to have slept on one.

The crowns were often discovered when a family member would lie down on their dead loved one's pillow and notice an uncomfortable knot. Unable to smooth out the lumpy knot, they would open the pillow to fix the issue, at which point they would discover the mysterious and unexplainable form of a crown inside. The crowns would shape into a very tight, neat bundle, with the quills pointing to the center of the crown.

Over time, many people began to believe that the death crowns were a sign from above that the person who had passed away had made it to heaven—that they'd earned their eternal crown. Another belief was that if a crown were found in the pillow of someone who was still alive, that person was not long for this world.

Like many other pieces of lore passed down through the generations, the feather death crown has provided comfort for many folks and has struck fear in the hearts of others. The Museum of Appalachia in Clinton, Tennessee, has a display dedicated to these crowns with samples of the phenomenon.

Sitting Up with the Dead

The practice of sitting up with the dead began in the days before funeral homes came to prominence. As most homes were quite rural, it was commonplace to have the visitation and funeral ceremony in one's home, with the body then being buried somewhere peaceful on the family's estate.

The deceased would be "laid out" in preparation for burial, as oftentimes the casket was a simple wooden box constructed from scratch at the home. The men would build the casket, and the women would sew together lining to be used inside it. Neighbors would pitch in their materials and labor at no charge to the family of the deceased.

The practice of sitting up with the dead began due to the lack of embalming that was available in most areas. A person (or rotation of people) would sit with the deceased to keep away flies, rodents and other pests that might be attracted to the corpse as it began to decay. The attending person would often be armed with a fly swatter or place a veil over the deceased as a layer of protection from infringing pests.

The human body occasionally does strange things once a person dies, and this has led to many frights down through the years. As creepy as sitting up with the dead seems to some people, it is exponentially creepier when the dead literally sit up by themselves. There have been numerous stories of a dead body mysteriously rising up in the casket, which understandably has caused much consternation for witnesses. The explanation for this unexpected (and unwelcome) turn of events is due to an excessive buildup of trapped gases in the body. If the body is in full rigor mortis (muscle stiffness), these trapped gases may expel themselves by making an eerie moaning or groaning sound. The job of sitting up with the dead put people at much greater risk of witnessing some of these body reactions, which makes the expense of using a funeral home seem far more reasonable in hindsight. The practice is virtually extinct these days, as access to proper burial methods has become more prevalent.

Holiday Superstitions

Holidays have inspired numerous superstitions and traditions in East Tennessee, and no holiday is more revered than Christmas. Christmas has unique customs specific to the season. Here are just a few examples:

- If you take a seat under a pine tree on Christmas Day, you will be able to hear angels singing. The downside to this is that it also means you will not live through the next year before departing this earth for your heavenly reward.
- A cat meowing on Christmas Day portends the appearance of evil spirits sometime in the upcoming year.

- Conversely, a crowing rooster on Christmas Eve will scare away evil spirits.
- Similarly, firing a gun into the air and setting off fireworks also helps scare away spooks.
- Coal and ash from a fire should not be thrown out on Christmas Day or it will bring a curse on the spirit of loved ones who have passed away.
- You should never take down a Christmas tree before January 2, but the tree must be taken down before the next December 6 to avoid bad luck.

New Year's Day brings its own special traditions, including a meal that is widespread in East Tennessee to ring in the New Year. It is customary throughout much of Appalachia to eat black-eyed peas and greens (either collard, mustard or turnip) for good luck and prosperity on New Year's Day. There are a few variations to this practice, as some say that you need to include a pork product in cooking the peas, while others say it needs to be served with cornbread.

The practice in the South supposedly dates back to the Civil War, when the troops of Union general William T. Sherman pillaged and plundered many areas of the South on his march to Atlanta. Sherman's troops thought they took or destroyed all of the usable food but left behind the black-eyed peas, unaware of their nutritional value. Southern people ate the peas to make it through the winter months and began to see the peas as a sign of good luck.

Many participants in this tradition say that you need to eat exactly 365 peas to ensure good luck throughout the year. If you come up short of 365, you will not have good fortune on an equal number of days in the year. If you eat more than 365, it will subtract your days with good luck by an equal amount to the number you go over.

The peas themselves are said by some to represent coins, while the greens stand for the "green" in dollar bills. People who add cornbread to the meal do so in the belief that it signifies gold. The pork is added for multiple reasons—pigs have long been seen as a sign of health and wealth in the South. Pigs also are known for their inability to turn their heads around fully to look backward, so some say it means they are always looking ahead to the future.

Death, Sickness and Good/Bad Luck Superstitions

Appalachians have had a long history of mountain superstitions tied to death, illness and misfortune to which many adhere religiously. Some are spooky and many are silly, but here is a list of a few omens and superstitions:

- If a bird flies into your house, death will soon come to someone in the household.
- If you dream about a birth, there will be a death, but if you dream about a death, then there will be a birth.
- If you walk on someone's grave, you will be haunted by their ghost.
- The sound of wind chimes calls up the dead.
- Death comes in threes; if one person dies, then two more are sure to follow.
- If a person's picture falls off the wall, that person will soon die.
- An owl hooting in the daytime means there's going to be a death soon.
- Cow moos after midnight means someone in the family will soon die.
- It is bad luck to rock an empty rocking chair.
- You must stop a swing yourself after getting off it; if the swing stops on its own, then death will soon come.
- It is bad luck to walk under a ladder.
- You must carry a body to be buried feet first or the spirit will return.
- If you hear a knock at the door and no one is there, it was a death knock warning you that someone is about to die.
- When someone leaves your home going on a trip, don't watch them until they get out of sight. If you do, they will never return.
- If you have a wart, take your neighbor's used dishrag and rub it on the wart. Then go bury the dirty rag at the nearest fork of the road, and the wart will be gone.
- Whoever opens a pocket knife should be the one to close it.
- If you spill salt, throw some over your left shoulder to prevent bad luck.
- If you spin a chair on one leg, it will give you bad luck.
- A whistling woman and a crowing hen always come to a bad end.
- If someone sweeps under your feet, you will never get married.
- If you break a mirror, you will have seven years of bad luck.
- If a black cat crosses in front of your car, you have to make an *X* on your windshield to avoid being cursed with bad luck.
- If you find a red cardinal feather, it will bring you good luck.

- If you have a bad dream, don't tell anyone any details about it before breakfast or it will come true.
- It is bad luck to open an umbrella inside a house.
- Never accept a free knife; you must at least pay the giver a penny for it to avoid bad luck.
- If you drop a biscuit when you remove a batch from the oven, you will have an unwelcome guest.
- If you sneeze before breakfast on Sunday morning, you will hear of a death before the week is over.
- If you find a cricket in your house and set it safely free outside, you will have good luck.
- If you feel a random shiver in your body, it means a rabbit or possum just crossed over the spot where your grave will be located.
- If you move into a new home, do not bring your old broom or mop to the new home lest you be cursed with bad luck in the home.
- It will bring bad luck to walk into a new home with one shoe on and one shoe off.
- You should always leave someone's house through the same door you entered to avoid bad luck.

HOME REMEDIES

There are several names that are commonly used for people who practice non-traditional forms of healing. In different cultures, you might hear reference to terms such as "witch doctor," "medicine man" or "shaman." Mountain people also have a name for their non-traditional home remedy healers in Appalachia: they are usually called "mamaw," "granny" or "nana." It's that little gray-haired lady in your life who can cure every ailment from a broken heart to the flu. Unlike most other healers who are shrouded in mystery and secretiveness, grannies are usually quick to dispense their vast knowledge of how to "cure what ails ya." In more recent years, the term "granny witches" has come into vogue for describing these practitioners of mountain medicine. Many granny witches are able to cure thrush in an infant by blowing directly into the baby's mouth. The ability to cure such illness is considered a gift that only a few chosen people are granted by divine ordination. Many such beliefs have been passed down for generations, primarily through immigrants of a Scotch-Irish lineage.

Home remedies have traditionally been popular in East Tennessee due to the lack of access to and expense of more traditional medicines. One of the most popular home remedies is a simple mixture for an Appalachian hot toddy to cure a nagging cough. It consists of mixing a shot of moonshine with a tablespoon of honey and a teaspoon of lemon juice. Warming this brew up is said to create a concoction that will stop a cough while helping you get a peaceful night's sleep. A word of caution: if you mess up the ratios in this formula and end up using a disproportionate amount of 'shine you may also "put hair on your chest" and a burning sensation in your throat.

Despite being in the heart of the Bible Belt, moonshine and other whiskey often get a free pass when being used for medicinal purposes. Some of the most vehemently anti-alcohol people in East Tennessee will suspend that disdain when it comes to mountain medicine. A classic exaggerated example of this is the character of Granny on *The Beverly Hillbillies*, who would take a swig of "white lightnin'" as a remedy for her rheumatism. Three of the most common ingredients that you will find in Appalachian home remedies are honey, vinegar and whiskey.

Another old mountain favorite, lye soap, is frequently cited as a cure-all for many skin ailments. Lye soap is made by combining lard (or other animal fat), lye and water. Old-fashioned lye soap has been used in East Tennessee households for treating acne, outbreaks of poison ivy and oak, sunburns and insect bites. Lye soap has also been used as a bug repellent, for removing stains from cloth and as bait for catching catfish.

There are home remedies to treat most any common illness, including colds, bronchitis, congestion, arthritis and joint pain, fever and so on. Poultices are made from varied ingredients, with very few people using the exact same formula and proportions to concoct their home brews. There are, however, some commonly held beliefs about the healing powers of certain vegetables and herbs. For example, onions are widely believed to absorb toxins and bacteria, which make them a lead ingredient in many poultices. Some people will cut up an onion and place it at the bottom of snug socks or left out in a bowl on a nightstand before going to bed to ward off illness. It has also been a common practice to chop up an onion for use as a natural air purifier in the home. Many people will not eat an onion a day or two after it has been cut open for fear of being poisoned by whatever toxin or bacteria it might have already absorbed. As evidence this isn't an entirely Appalachian idea, it has been suggested that the English in Great Britain used onions to combat the Black Death plague during the Middle Ages.

Some other common home remedy ingredients are garlic, turpentine, lard, mustard, honey and even tobacco. Garlic is said to have many of the same toxin-fighting benefits of onions. Turpentine and lard have been combined for use in many remedies for joint pain. A "mustard plaster" remedy is made by taking four tablespoons of dry mustard, mixing with lard and then spreading it onto a piece of flannel cloth to be heated in an oven before being placed on a congested person's chest. Tobacco is placed on insect bites to take out the sting and itch of them.

Although most of these remedies are scoffed at by modern medicine, a handful of them have recently rebounded in popularity. Honey has long been a primary ingredient in many home remedies, and more recently, science has agreed with its usefulness as a healing agent. Honey is now frequently used to combat allergies; for its qualities as an antioxidant, as a cough suppressant and as a sleep aid; to treat burns and other wounds; as a memory booster; and even as an ingredient for an all-natural energy drink.

Another folk remedy that has seen a recent rejuvenation is the use of gin-soaked raisins for pain relief in the treatment of arthritis. The simple formula is to pour just enough gin over a bowl full of raisins to cover their top. Wait until the gin is completely evaporated (which can take up to a week) and then put them in a mason jar for storage. A person afflicted with arthritis can then consume up to ten of the raisins per day to combat chronic pain. The juniper berries used in the making of gin have long been used for medicinal purposes dating back to the Greeks and Romans. These juniper berries are thought to have antioxidant and antibacterial properties. The process of making raisins leaves behind sulfides on the grapes, which are thought to be useful for their anti-inflammatory benefits. The gin-soaked raisins combine the antioxidant, antibacterial and anti-inflammatory benefits of the gin and raisins into one great-tasting raisin "pill." This remedy was brought to national consciousness by the late radio personality Paul Harvey, who described the gin-soaked raisins on his program one day and then had numerous listeners call in speaking of all the wonderful benefits they enjoyed from taking them.

Home remedies have remained popular through the years, even if they don't always get the backing of the medical community. Whether some of their success is due to true medicinal benefits or just because people expect them to work, there are many people of East Tennessee who still swear by them.

Selected Bibliography

Abramson, Rudy, Jean Haskell and Michael Lofaro. *Encyclopedia of Appalachia.* Knoxville: University of Tennessee Press, 2006.

Alderman, Pat. *Dragging Canoe: Cherokee-Chickamauga War Chief.* Johnson City, TN: Overmountain Press, 1978.

Bakeless, John. *Daniel Boone: Master of the Wilderness.* Lincoln: University of Nebraska Press, 1989.

Bender, Margaret. *Signs of Cherokee Culture: Sequoyah's Syllabary in Eastern Cherokee Life.* Chapel Hill: University of North Carolina Press, 2002.

Burton, Thomas. *Serpent-Handling Believers.* Knoxville: University of Tennessee Press, 1993.

Cavender, Anthony. *Folk Medicine in Southern Appalachia.* Chapel Hill: University of North Carolina Press, 2003.

Crockett, David. *A Narrative of the Life of David Crockett.* Baltimore, MD: E.L. Carey and A. Hart, 1834.

Davidson, Donald. *The Tennessee: The Old River, Frontier to Secession.* Nashville, TN: J.S. Sanders & Company, 1991.

Driver, Carl. *John Sevier: Pioneer of the Old Southwest.* Chapel Hill: University of North Carolina Press, 1932.

Elder, Pat Spurlock. *Melungeons: Examining an Appalachian Legend.* Blountville, TN: Continuity Press, 1999.

Faragher, John Mack. *Daniel Boone: The Life and Legend of an American Pioneer.* New York: Holt, 1992.

Foreman, Grant. *Sequoyah.* Norman: University of Oklahoma Press, 1938.

Fulgham, Richard Lee. *Appalachian Genesis: The Clinch River Valley from Prehistoric Times to the End of the Frontier Era.* Johnson City, TN: Overmountain Press, 2000.

Groneman, Bill. *Death of a Legend: The Myth and Mystery Surrounding the Death of Davy Crockett.* Plano: Republic of Texas Press, 1999.

Hood, Ralph W., Jr., and W. Paul Williamson. *Them that Believe: The Power and the Meaning of the Christian Serpent-Handling Tradition.* Berkeley: University of California Press, 2008.

Kennedy, N. Brent, and Robyn Vaughan Kennedy. *The Melungeons: The Resurrection of a Proud People, an Untold Story of Ethnic Cleansing in America.* 2nd ed. Macon, GA: Mercer University Press, 1997.

Langsdon, Phillip. *Tennessee: A Political History.* Franklin, TN: Hillboro Press, 2000.

Lee, David D. *Sergeant York: An American Hero.* Lexington: University Press of Kentucky, 1985.

Michno, Gregory, and Susan Michno. *Circle the Wagons!: Attacks on Wagon Trains in History and Hollywood Films.* Jefferson, NC: McFarland, 2008.

Mooney, James. *Myths of the Cherokee and Sacred Formulas of the Cherokee.* Nashville, TN: Charles and Randy Elder-Booksellers, 1982.

Moran, Mark, and Mark Sceurman. *Weird U.S.: Your Travel Guide to America's Local Legends and Best Kept Secrets.* New York: Sterling Publishing Company Inc., 2009.

Olson, Ted. *The Hanging of Mary, a Circus Elephant.* Knoxville: University of Tennessee Press, 2009.

Olwell, Russell. *At Work in the Atomic City: A Labor and Social History of Oak Ridge, Tennessee.* Knoxville: University of Tennessee Press, 2004.

Price, Charles Edwin. *The Day They Hung the Elephant.* Johnson City, TN: Overmountain Press, 1992.

———. *Haunted Jonesborough.* Johnson City, TN: Overmountain Press, 1993.

Richmond, Nancy. *Appalachian Folklore Omens, Signs and Superstitions.* N.p.: CreateSpace Independent Publishing Platform, 2011.

Schlosser, S.E.E., and Paul Hoffman. *Spooky South: Tales of Hauntings, Strange Happenings, and Other Local Lore.* Guilford, CT: Globe Pequot Press, 2011.

Steely, Michael S. *Swift's Silver Mines and Related Appalachian Treasures.* Johnson City, TN: Overmountain Press, 1995.

Swanson, Neil. *More Odd & Peculiar: Unusual Town Names in all Fifty States from Arundel, Maine to Zigzag, Oregon.* River Falls, WI: Wainsley Press, 1999.

Taylor, Troy. *Beyond the Grave: The History of America's Most Haunted Graveyards.* N.p.: Whitechapel Productions, 2001.

———. *Spirits of the Civil War*. N.p.: Whitechapel Production, 1999.

Toropov, Brandon. *The Complete Idiot's Guide to Urban Legends*. N.p.: Alpha Books, 2001.

Wallis, Michael. *David Crockett: The Lion of the West*. New York: W.W. Norton & Company, 2011.

Westcott, Ed. *Oak Ridge*. Charleston, SC: Arcadia Publishing, 2005.

Wheeler, Richard. *Sergeant York and the Great War*. Bulverde, TX: Mantle Ministries, 1998.

White, Peter. *Encyclopedia of Appalachia*. Knoxville: University of Tennessee Press, 2006.

About the Author

Shane Simmons is a founder of The Appalachian Project (TAP), a multimedia group created to preserve the heritage of the Central and Southern Appalachians. He has more than twenty years of experience in the financial services industry and is a lifelong resident of the Appalachian Mountains. Simmons received his undergraduate degree in business management from Emory and Henry College in Emory, Virginia. In addition to East Tennessee folklore, his areas of interest include the history of the coal mining industry in Central Appalachia, the Civil War in East Tennessee and Southwest Virginia and Appalachian cultural history.